Empire, Capitalism, and Democracy

Empire, Capitalism, and Democracy

The Early American Experience

Edited by Kyle G. Volk and Patrick Mulford O'Connor

The University of Montana

cognella®

SAN DIEGO

Bassim Hamadeh, CEO and Publisher
Kristina Stolte, Acquisitions Editor
Alisa Munoz, Project Editor
Berenice Quirino, Associate Production Editor
Jess Estrella, Senior Graphic Designer
Trey Soto, Licensing Coordinator
Natalie Piccotti, Director of Marketing
Kassie Graves, Vice President of Editorial
Jamie Giganti, Director of Academic Publishing

Cover image copyright© Henry Bryan Hall, "The Battle of New Orleans." N.P. Fitzpatrick, 1861.

Printed in the United States of America.

3970 Sorrento Valley Blvd., Ste. 500, San Diego, CA 92121

Contents

To our parents

INTRODUCTION

This book documents the history of the United States from the opening of the Atlantic World to the post–Civil War era. It contains nearly thirty primary sources created by women and men who lived during these centuries. These sources' genres, like their creators, are diverse: they include petitions, personal correspondences, speeches, essays, and cartoons. Despite these differences, each document reflects aspects of the relevant concerns of the era in which it was produced.

We have selected these documents because they illustrate three interdependent forces that animated the history of early America: empire, capitalism, and democracy. These forces were the product of human decision-making. None of them existed outside of significant challenges. Each of them changed over time. When brought together, they capture central themes in early American history.

By *empire*, we mean the expansion of one political entity's territorial claims, access to resources and markets, and governing authority over land and peoples at the expense of other political entities' territory, wealth, and power. In this book, the political entities in question include the United States; major European powers such as Great Britain, France, and Spain; and Native American tribes and confederacies throughout North America.

By *capitalism*, we mean the economic choices and the social and political structures that organized people's trade interactions within markets; transformed land, goods, and even humans into commodities that could be bought or sold for a price; and encouraged the investment of wealth in ventures, such as the Atlantic slave trade in the eighteenth century or the construction of factories in the nineteenth century, with the promise of future profits.

By *democracy*, we mean the system of government and social order that Americans instituted to replace European systems of monarchy. Democracy rested on theoretical commitments to human equality, individual rights, and popular sovereignty, or the right of the people to rule. It also encompassed dynamic political practices—from constitution making and voting to partisan politics and social reform—that involved a wide range of Americans in public life.

Because the following documents are primary sources, it is essential to avoid imposing our twenty-first-century expectations upon them. To aid your historical thinking, begin by answering several essential questions about each document. First, what was the context of its creation? To aid your contextualization of the documents, we have provided a brief introduction for each chapter. Second, what caused the author to come to his or her conclusions, and what consequences may those conclusions have had for the author's contemporaries? Finally, what other perspectives coexisted and perhaps conflicted with the author's? You will not exhaustively answer any of these questions, but asking them will help you illuminate the significance of each document.

As you read these documents, keep two central goals in mind: first, to comprehend them, and second, to be able to engage in thoughtful conversation about them. To help you achieve these goals, we have provided questions for each chapter. As you will see, most chapters divide questions under two headings: "Fundamentals" and "Analysis and Interpretation." We intend "Fundamentals" to aid your basic comprehension of each reading, including your ability to identify each author's key goals, arguments, and approach. Questions for "Analysis and Interpretation" will encourage you to critically interrogate the texts for historical significance. Ground your responses to these questions in evidence drawn from the readings. Your answers will likely differ from others engaging with the texts. Those differences will enable you and others to engage in discussions that should unsettle, complicate, and strengthen your understanding of early American history.

Finally, recognize that this book is a tool meant to aid your learning. It is yours, so underline important passages, take notes in the margins, prepare responses under the questions, and write down your own questions as you go. Successful study of the past requires this type of active engagement. Enjoy the adventure.

PART I

The Opening of the Atlantic World

CHAPTER 1

Contact, Exchange, and Conquest

At the time of European contact, the Americas were among the most populated and diverse regions in the world. North America, South America, and the Caribbean islands were ancient homelands to millions of people. Their residents spoke hundreds of languages and developed complex systems of governance, religion, and trade. The Americas sustained a wide range of communities, including the massive, urbanized Aztec and Inca societies of present-day Mexico and Peru and the smaller agricultural and hunting communities of the present-day United States.

The image below illustrates European assumptions about the people and environment they encountered in the Americas. Drawn by the artist Stradanus circa 1587 and engraved by Theodoor Galle roughly a decade later, the image depicts Italian explorer Amerigo Vespucci's "discovery" of America. Vespucci had voyaged to South America in 1499 and 1502 and was the first European to proclaim that the landmasses to Europe's west were not Asia but an entirely different continent.

ANALYSIS AND INTERPRETATION

1. How did Stradanus portray the peoples and environment of the "New World"?

2. What might this portrayal suggest about the "Old World"?

3. Why might Stradanus have portrayed the most prominent American inhabitant as a female?

4. Based on this portrayal, what prospects might Europeans have anticipated in the colonization of the New World?

5. If an indigenous American artist depicted this same subject, what would be different? What would be the same?

6. If you were to analyze this image further, what other information might be helpful? Why?

FIGURE 1.1   Amerigo Vespuccio et l'Amerique

Credit

CHAPTER 2

Roots of English Empire and "New World" Civilizations

The European explorers who "discovered" North and South America at the end of the fifteenth century (the 1400s) spurred a major European reorientation toward the west. In the sixteenth century, the Catholic power Spain took the lead. With support from the Spanish crown, Spanish conquistadores explored the "New World" and founded colonies in various parts of the Caribbean and mainland North and South America. With the essential aid of Old World diseases, Spanish colonizers violently subdued Native American peoples and forced those who survived to engage in grueling labor, most notoriously in gold and silver mines. By the mid-sixteenth century, the Spanish crown had become the richest in Europe, and the Spanish Empire had become among the world's most powerful. New World conquest, it seemed, offered boundless possibilities for prosperity and power.

Unlike Spain, England stayed on the sidelines of New World exploration and empire in the sixteenth century. Religious squabbles born of the Protestant Reformation as well as colonization efforts in Ireland kept England distracted. By the final third of the century, however, influential voices in English society began to push for England's entrance into the game of New World colonies. Foremost among them was a writer, geographer, and Anglican minister named Richard Hakluyt (1552–1616). In 1584, Hakluyt wrote "A Discourse Concerning Western Planting" to convince Queen Elizabeth I (England's monarch) to support colonization and to encourage wealthy Englishmen to invest in colonial enterprises.

By the time Roger Williams published *A Key into the Language* of America some sixty years later, England had established several colonial footholds in North America. Williams was among the many religious dissenters called Puritans who journeyed across the Atlantic in the 1630s to launch a religious utopia. Puritans hoped their colony would stand in sharp contrast to the perceived corruptions of the Catholic Church and England's Anglican Church. Though a Puritan minister himself, Williams was banished from Massachusetts for criticizing the punishment of religious dissenters and for insisting that colonists purchase Indian lands before occupying them. Williams quickly established Providence Plantation (what would become Rhode Island) and continued to spend substantial time with local Native Americans. He published his observations of the language and culture of the Narragansetts in 1643. *A Key into the Language of America* was the first study of Indian culture written in English, and its publication brought Williams attention in England as an important analyst of the New World and its peoples.

FUNDAMENTALS

The following primary sources are particularly rich and should raise numerous questions for you. While reading these documents—and all subsequent documents in this book—be sure to consider these basic questions:

1. What was the purpose of this document?

2. Who were the intended audiences?

3. How might the intended purposes and audiences have shaped the document?

ANALYSIS AND INTERPRETATION

1. Do the themes of Stradanus's Vespucci painting (from Chapter 1) echo in these two documents? How so?

2. What assumptions did Hakluyt hold about Native Americans, English colonists, and the New World environment? How might the intent of Hakluyt's document have influenced his characterizations?

3. How did the shadow of the Spanish Empire loom over Hakluyt's case for colonization? What might have been the consequences for England if it decided to forego colonial enterprises?

4. Did Roger Williams think European culture was superior to Native American civilization?

5. To what extent was Roger Williams optimistic about future relations between the English and Native Americans?

Richard Hakluyt, "A Discourse Concerning Western Planting" (1584)[1]

A brief collection of certain reasons to induce her Majesty and the state to take in hand the western voyage and the planting there.

1. The soil yieldth and may be made to yield all the several commodities of Europe, and of all kingdomes, dominions, and territories that England tradeth with that by trade of merchandise cometh into this realm.

2. The passage thither and home is neither to long nor to short but easy and to be made twice in the year. ...

5. And where England now for certain hundreth years last passed, by the peculiar commodity of wools, and of later years by clothing of the same, hath raised itself from meaner state to greatr wealth and much highr honour, mighty and power than before, to the equaling of the princes of the same to the greatst potentates of this part of the world it cometh now so to passe, that by the great endeavour of the increase of the trade of wools in Spain and in the West Indies, now daily more and more multiplying that the wools of England, and the clothe made of the same, will become base, and every day more base then other; which, prudently weighed yet behoveth this realm if it mean not to return to former olde means and baseness but to stand in present and late former honour, glory, and force, and not negligently and sleepingly to slide into beggery, to foresee and to plant at Norumbega [New England] or some like place, were it not for any thing else but for the hope of the vent of our wool endraped, the principal and in effect the only enriching continuing natural commodity of this realm. And effectually pursuing that course, we shall not only find on that tract of land, and especially in that firm northward (to whom warm clothe shall be right welcome), an ample vent, but also shall, from the north side of that firm, find out known and unknown islands and dominions replenished with people that may fully vent the abundance of that our commodity, that else will in few years wax of none or of small value by foreign abundance &c.; so as by this enterprise we shall shun the imminent mischief hanging over our heads that else must needs fall upon the realm without breach of peace or sword drawn against this realm by any foreign state; and not offer our ancient riches to scornful neighbors at home, nor sell the same in effect for nothing, as we shall shortly, if presently it be not provided for. ...

6. This enterprise may stay the Spanish King from flowing over all the face of that waste firm of America, if we seat and plant there in time, in time I say, and we by planting shall [prevent] him from making more short and more safe returns out of the noble ports of the purposed places of our planting, then by any possibility he can from the part of the firm that now his navys by ordinary courses come from, in this that there is no comparison between the ports of the coasts that the King of Spain doth now possess and use and the ports of the coasts that our nation is to possess by planting at Norumbega, ... And England possessing the purposed place of planting, her Majesty may, by the benefit of the seat having won good and royall havens, have

---

1   From Charles Deane, ed., *Documentary History of the State of Maine* Vol. II (Cambridge, 1877), 152–161.

plenty of excellent trees for masts of goodly timber to build ships and to make great navys, of pitch, tar, hemp, and all things incident for a navy royall, and that for no price, and without money or request. How easy a matter may yet be to this realm, swarming at this day with valiant youths, rusting and hurtful by lack of employment, and having good makers of cable and of all sorts of cordage, and the best and most cunning shipwrights of the world, to be lords of all those seas, and to spoil Phillip's Indian navy, and to deprive him of yearly passage of his treasure into Europe, and consequently to abate the pride of Spain and of the suporter of the great Anti-Christ of Rome and to pull him down in equality to his neighbour princes, and consequently to cut of the common mischiefs that come to all Europe by the peculiar abundance of his Indian treasure, and this without difficulty.

7. ... this realm shall have by that mean ships of great burden and of great strength for the defense of this realm, and for the defense of that new seat as need shall require, and with all great increase of perfect seamen, which great princes in time of wars want, and which kind of men are neither nourished in few days nor in few years ...

10. No foreign commodity that comes into England comes without payment of custom once, twice, or thrice, before it come into the realm, and so all foreign commodities become dearer to the subjects of this realm; and by this course to Norumbega foreign princes customs are avoided; and the foreign commodities cheaply purchased, they become cheap to the subjects of England, to the common benefit of the people, and to the saving of great treasure in the realm; whereas now the realm become the poor by the purchasing of foreign commodities in so great a mass at so excessive prices.

11. At the first traffic with the people of those parts, the subjects of this realm for many years shall change many cheap commodities of these parts for things of high valor there not esteemed; and this to the great enriching of the *realm,* if common use fail not.

12. By the great plenty of those regions the merchants and their factors shall lie there cheap, buy and repair their ships cheap, and shall return at pleasure without stay or restraint of foreign prince; whereas upon stays and restraints the merchant raiseth his charge in sale over of his ware; and, buying his wares cheap, he may maintain trade with small stock, and without taking up money upon interest; and so he shall be rich and not subject to many hazards, but shall be able to afford the commodities for cheap prices to all subjects of the realm.

13. By making of ships and by preparing of things for the same, by making of cables and cordage, by planting of vines and olive trees, and by making of wine and oil, by husbandry, and by thousands of things there to be done, infinite numbers of the English nation may be set on work, to the unburdening of the realm with many that now live chargeable to the state at home.

14. If the sea coast serve for making of salt, and the inland for wine, oils, oranges, lemons, figs, &c., and for making of iron, all which with much more is hoped, without sword drawn, we shall cut the comb of the French, of the Spanish, of the Portingal, and of enemies, and of doubtful friends, to the abating of their wealth and force, and to the great saving of the wealth of the realm. ...

16. Wee shall by planting there enlarge the glory of the gospel, and from England plant sincere religion, and provide a safe and a sure place to receive people from all parts of the world that are forced to flee for the truth of God's word.

17. If frontier wars there chance to arise, and if thereupon we shall fortify, yet will occasion the training up of our youth in the discipline of war, and make a number fit for the service of the wars and for the defense of our people there and at home.

18. The Spaniards govern in the Indies with all pride and tyranny; and like as when people of contrary nature at the sea enter into gallies, where men are tied as slaves, all yell and cry with one voice, *Liberta, liberta,* as desirous of liberty and freedom, so no doubt whensoever the Queen of England, a prince of such clemency, shall seat upon that firm of America, and shall be reported throughout all that tract to use the natural people there with all humanity, curtesy, and freedom, they will yield themselves to her government, and revolt clean from the Spaniard, and specially when they shall understand that she hath a noble navy, and that she aboundeth with a people most valiant for their defense. And her Majesty having Sir Frances Drake and other subjects already in credit with the Symerons, a people or great multitude already revolted from the Spanish government, she may with them and a few hundreths of this nation, trained up in the late wars of France and Flanders, bring great things to pass, and that with great ease; and this brought so about, her Majesty and her subjects may both enjoy the treasure of the mines of gold and silver, and the whole trade and all the gain of the trade of merchandisse, that now passeth thither by the Spaniards only hand, of all the commodities of Europe; which trade of merchandise only were of it self sufficient (without the benefit of the rich mine) to enrich the subjects, and by customs to fill her Majesty's coffers to the full. And if it be high policy to maintain the poor people of this realm in work, I dare affirm that if the poor people of England were five times so many as they be, yet all might be set on work in and by working linen, and such other things of merchandise as the trade into the Indies doth require.

19. The present short trades causeth the mariner to be cast of, and often to be idle, and so by poverty to fall to piracy. But this course to Norumbega being longer, and a continuance of the employment of the mariner, doth keep the mariner from idleness and from necessity; and so it cutteth of the principal actions of piracy, and the rather because no riche pray for them to take cometh directly in their course or any thing near their course.

20. Many men of excellent wits and of divers singular gifts, overthrown by ... by some folly of youth, that are not able to live in England, may there be raised again, and do their country good service; and many needful uses there may (to great purpose) require the saving of great numbers, that for trifles may otherwise be devoured by the gallows.

21. Many soldiers and servitors, in the end of the wars, that might be hurtful to this *realm,* may there be unladen, to the common profit and quiet of this *realm,* and to our foreign benefit there, as they may be employed.

22. The frye [children] of the wandering beggars of England, that grow up idly, and hurteful and burdenous to this *realm,* may there be unladen, better bred up, and may people waste countries to the home and foreign benefit, and to their own more happy state.

23. If England cry out and affirm, that there is so many in all trades that one cannot live for another, as in all places they doe, this Norumbega (if it be thought so good) offereth the remedy.

Roger Williams, *A Key into the Language of America* (1643)[2]

The natives are of two sorts (as the English are) some more rude and clownish, who are not so apt to salute, but upon salutation resalute lovingly. Others, and the general, are *sober* and *grave*, and yet chearfull in a meane, and as ready to begin a Salutation as to Resalute, which yet the English generally begin, out of desire to civilize them. ... There is a favour of *civility* and *courtesie* even amongst these wild Americans, both amongst *themselves* and towards *strangers*. ...

Whomsoever commeth in when they are eating, they offer them to eat of that which they have, though but little enough prepar'd for themselves. If any provision of *fish* or *flesh* come in, they make their neighbours partakers with them.

If any stranger come in, they presently give him to eate of what they have; many a time, and at all times of the night (as I have fallen in travel upon their houses) when nothing hath been ready, have themselves and their wives, risen to prepare me some refreshing. ...

It is a strange *truth*, that a man shall generally finde more free entertainment and refreshing amongst these *Barbarians*, then amongst thousands that call themselves *Christians*. ...

Having no Letters nor Arts, 'tis admirable how quick they are in casting up great numbers, with the helpe of grains of Corne, instead of *Europes* pens or counters. ...

Their *affections*, especially to their children, are very strong; so that I have known a Father take so grievously the losse of his *childe*, that hee hath cut and stob'd himselfe with *griefe* and *rage*.

This extreme *affection*, together with want of *learning*, makes their children sawcie, bold, and undutiful.

I once came into a *house*, and requested some *water* to drinke; the *father* bid his sonne (of some 8. yeeres of age) to fetch some *water*: the *boy* refused, and would not stir; I told the *father* that I would correct my *child*, if he should so disobey me, &c. Upon this the *father* took up a sticke, the *boy* another, and flew at his *father*: upon my perswasion, the poore *father* made him smart a little, throw down his stick, and run for *water*, and the *father* confessed the benefit of *correction*, and the evill of their too indulgent *affections*.

They are as full of businesse, and as impatient of hinderance (in their kind) as any Merchant in *Europe*. ...

Their women constantly beat all their corne with hand: they plant it, dresse it, gather it, barne it, beat it, and take as much paines as any people in the world, which labour is questionlesse one cause of their extraordinary ease of child birth.

Whence they call *English-men* Chauquaquock, that is, *Knive-men*, stone formerly being to them in stead of *Knives*, *Awle-blades*, *Hatchets and Howes*.

It is almost incredible what burthens the poore women carry of *Corne*, of *Fish*, of *Beanes*, of *Mats*, and a childe besides. ...

---

2   From Roger Williams, *A Key into the Language of America* (London: Gregory Dexter, 1643), 27, 32, 36–37, 42, 45–46, 50, 51, 58, 62, 63, 64, 65, 73, 75, 86, 89, 106, 121, 128, 129, 135, 137.

Yet some cut their haire round, and some as low and as short as the sober *English*; yet I never saw any so to forget nature it selfe in such excessive length and monstrous fashion, as to the shame of the *English* Nation, I now (with griefe) see my Country-men in *England* are degenerated unto. ...

Their desire of, and delight in newes, is great, as the *Athenians*, and all men, more or lesse; a stranger that can relate newes in their owne language, they will stile him *Manittoo*, a God.

Their Manner is upon any tidings to sit round, double or treble, or more, as their numbers be; I have seene neer a thousand in a round, where *English* could not well neere halfe so many have sitten: Every man hath his pipe of their *Tobacco*, and a depe silence they make, and attention give to him that speaketh; and many of them will deliver themselves, either in a relation of news, or in a consultation, with very emphatically speech and great action, commonly an houre, and sometimes two houres together. ...

As one answered me when I had discoursed about many points of God, of the creation, of the soule, of the danger of it, and the saving of it, he assented; but when I spake of the rising againe of the boyd, he cryed out, I shall never believe this.

Canounicus, the old high *Sachim* of the *Nariganset Bay* (a wise and peaceable Prince) once in a solemne Oration to my selfe, in a solemne assembly ... said, I have never suffered any wrong to be offered to the *English* since they landed; nor never will: he often repeated this ... if the *Englishman* speake true, if hee meane truly, then shall I goe to my grave in peace, and hope that the *English* and my posteritie shall live in love and peace together. I replied, that he had no cause (as I hoped) to question *Englishmans* ... faithfulnesse, he having had long experience of their friendlinesse and trustinesse. He took a sticke, and broke it into ten pieces, and related ten instances (laying downe a sticke to every instance) which gave him cause thus to feare and say; I satisfied him in some presently, and presented the rest to the Governours of the *English*, who, I hope will be far from giving just cause to have *Barbarians* to question their ... faithfulnesse. ...

This question they oft put to me: Why come the *Englishmen* hither? And measuring others by themselves; they say, It is because you want *firing* for they, having burnt up the *wood* in one place ... and so to remove to a fresh new place for the *woods* sake. ...

I have heard of many *English* lost, and have oft been lost my selfe, and ... have often been found, and succoured by the *Indians*. ...

They are joyfull in meeting of any in travel, and will strike fire either with stones or sticks, to take Tobacco, and discourse a little together. ...

The *Indians* having abundance of these sorts of Foule upon their waters, take great pains to kill any of them with their Bow and Arrowes; and are marvelous desirous of our *English* Guns, powder, and shot (though they are wisely and generally denied by the *English*) yet with those which they get from the *French*, and some others (*Dutch* and *English*) they kill abundance of Fowle, being naturally excellent marks-men; and also more hardened to endure the weather, and wading, lying, and creeping on the ground, &c. ...

The *Natives* are very exact and punctuall in the bounds of their Lands, belonging to this or that Prince or People, (even to a River, Brooke &c.) And I have knowne them make bargaine and sale amongst themselves for a small piece, or quantity of Ground: notwithstanding a sinfull opinion amongst many that Christians have right to *Heathens* Lands ...

They have a two-fold nakednesse: First ordinary and constant, when although they have a Beasts skin, or an English mantle on, yet that covers ordinarily but their hinder parts and all the foreparts from top to toe, (except their secret parts, covered with a little Apron, after the patterne of their and our first Parents) I say all else open and naked.

Their male children goe starke naked, and have no Apron untill they come to ten or twelve yeers of age; their Female they, in a modest blush cover with a little Apron of an hand breadth from their very birth. Their second nakednesse is when their men oftern abroad, and both men and women within doors, leave off their beasts skin, or English cloth, and so (excepting their little Apron) are wholly naked; yet but few of the women but will keepe their skin or cloth (though loose) neare to them ready to gather it up about them.

Custome hath used their minds and bodies to it, and in such a freedom from any wantonesse, that I have never seen that wantonesses amongst them, as, (with griefe) I have heard of in *Europe* ...

I could never discerne that excesse of scandalous sins amongst them, which *Europe* aboundeth with. Drunkennesse and gluttony, generally they know not what sinnes they be; and although they have not so much to restraine them (both in respect of knowledge of God and Lawes of Men) as the *English* have, yet a man shall never heare of such crimes amongst them of robberies, murthers, adulteries, &c. as amongst the *English* ...

The *Indians* bring downe all their sorts of Furs, which they take in the Countrey, both to the *Indians* and to the *English* for this *Indian Money* [Wampum]: this Money the *English*, *French*, and *Dutch*, trade to the Indians, six hundred miles in severall parts (North and South from *New-England*) for their Furres, and whatsoever they stand in need of from them: as Corne, Venison, &c. ...

This one fathom of this their stringed money, now worth of the English but five shillings (sometimes more) some few yeeres since was worthy nine, and sometimes ten shillings *per* Fathome: the fall is occasioned by the fall of Beaver in *England*: the Natives are very impatient, when for English commodities they pay so much more of their money, and not understanding the cause of it; and many say the English cheat and deceive them, though I have labored to make them understand the reason of it. ...

Who ever deale or trade with them, had need of Wisedom, Patience, and Faithfulnesse in dealing: for they frequently say ... you lye ... you deceive. ...

O the infinite wisedome of the most holy wise *God*, who hath so advanced *Europe*, above *America*, that there is not a sorry *Howe*, *Hatchet*, *Knife*, nor a rag of cloth in all *America*, but what comes over the dreadfull *Atlantick* Ocean from *Europe*: and yet that *Europe* be not proud, nor *America* discouraged. What treasures are hid in some parts of *America*, and in our *New-English* parts, how have foule hands (in smoakie houses) the first handling of those Furres which are after worne upon the hands of Queens and heads of Princes.

CHAPTER 3

The Slave Trade and the Atlantic World, Part 1

Consider the questions in this chapter while reading the first half of historian Randy Sparks's book, *The Two Princes of Calabar: An Eighteenth-Century Atlantic Odyssey* (pages 1–69). Please identify passages from the book to support your answers.

FUNDAMENTALS

1. Why is *Two Princes of Calabar* considered a "secondary source," while the documents from Chapter 2 (Hakluyt and Williams) are considered "primary sources"?

2. Who is historian Randy Sparks's intended audience, and how might that audience have shaped the book that he has written?

ANALYSIS AND INTERPRETATION

1. To what extent were the Robin Johns typical of the African experience in the eighteenth-century Atlantic World? In what ways were they exceptional?

2. What does the expression "Atlantic Creoles" mean? How does the idea of "Atlantic Creoles" help Sparks explain the world that the Robin Johns inhabited?

3. Why was the Old Town Massacre of 1767 such an important turning point? In what ways was this historical event important for historian Randy Sparks?

4. How does Sparks explain the participation of Africans in the African slave trade? How does Sparks differentiate between slavery in Africa and slavery in the New World?

5. On page 58, historian Randy Sparks states that Efik culture "became increasingly commodified" as the slave trade grew in importance. What does he mean by this? In what ways did the exchange of European goods for enslaved Africans shape Efik society?

CHAPTER 4

The Slave Trade and the Atlantic World, Part 2

Consider the questions in this chapter while reading the second half of historian Randy Sparks's book, *The Two Princes of Calabar: An Eighteenth-Century Atlantic Odyssey* (pages 70–147). Please identify passages from the book to support your answers.

FUNDAMENTALS

1. Historian Randy Sparks describes his history as a "microhistory." What does he mean by this?

2. What are the virtues of this style of history (microhistory)? What are its drawbacks?

ANALYSIS AND INTERPRETATION

1. What does the Robin Johns' story tell us about the impact of the opening of the Atlantic World on the continent of Africa and African peoples?

2. Historians of slavery are particularly interested in the concept of "agency"—the ability of the enslaved to shape their own lives and the world around them. Did the Robin Johns exercise agency while they were held as slaves? To what extent did their own agency facilitate their escape from slavery?

3. Was it easy to escape slavery in the late eighteenth-century Atlantic World? To what extent were the Robin Johns unique in their ability to escape slavery?

4. Why did the Robin Johns convert to Christianity? How should we characterize the relationship of the Atlantic slave trade to Protestantism in the eighteenth century?

5. In your assessment, who (and which groups of people) was most responsible for the slave trade? Why? How does Sparks's book shed light on this question?

6. Why did the Robin Johns return to the Atlantic slave trade? How does this affect our view of their responsibility? Can we say that the Robin Johns truly escaped slavery?

PART II

Revolutionary America

CHAPTER 5

The Contested American Revolution

When the Seven Years' War ended in 1763, feelings of loyalty and unity permeated British America. Despite the ocean between the colonies and the mother country, colonists believed they had contributed to the preservation of British liberty by driving Catholic France from North America. They were overwhelmingly proud to be part of the British Empire.

In the ensuing years, the socioeconomic order of colonial America deteriorated. A postwar economic decline wreaked havoc in urban seaports and rural farmlands. British tax and trade policies, intended to draw the colonies more firmly under the control of the British Empire, instead soured colonists' perceptions of the mother country. Nonetheless, even as aggrieved colonists took up arms in 1775, many continued to demand respect for their rights as British subjects. As they understood it, the British constitutional system was sound. It was the decisions of Parliament and King George III they protested.

The publication of Thomas Paine's *Common Sense* in January 1776 marked a turning point in America's revolutionary saga. Paine was born in England, but he threw himself behind the American cause after immigrating to Philadelphia in 1774. Rather than defend colonists' rights as British subjects, *Common Sense* argued that imperial governance of North America and even the concept of monarchy was illogical. Independence—and the creation of independent American governments rooted in the sovereignty of the people—was the only reasonable outcome. Written in an accessible style intended for a mass audience, Paine's pamphlet reached hundreds of thousands of readers and helped galvanize colonists in favor of independence.

Yet, as the selection from James Chalmers's *Plain Truth* indicates, not all colonists shared Paine's conclusions. For many, the ideas of liberty, prosperity, and security were synonymous with remaining part of the British Empire. As war engulfed the colonies, the opponents of independence faced the difficult choice of aligning themselves with a cause they rejected or endangering their livelihoods—or even their lives.

These two documents represent not only the different ideological interpretations of the American Revolution but also the life-or-death choices colonists faced as the conflict with Britain turned to war.

FUNDAMENTALS

1. What were Paine's criticisms of monarchy?

2. How did Paine respond to the Revolution's opponents?

3. Why, according to Paine, would the colonies flourish after independence?

4. What flaws did Chalmers identify in democratic governments?

5. What outcome did Chalmers predict would follow independence?

ANALYSIS AND INTERPRETATION

1. If we understand "radical" to mean "departing meaningfully from the usual," to what extent was Paine's indictment of monarchy and hereditary succession a radical act?

2. Why might *Common Sense* have been so convincing? Which aspects might have especially appealed to the more popular audience Paine hoped to reach?

3. Paine claimed that "The cause of America is in a great measure the cause of all mankind." What did he mean by this? What were the potential consequences of such a claim?

4. Why did Chalmers suggest that "Independence and Slavery Are Synonymous Terms"?

5. Paine suggested that independence would yield a prosperous and functioning society. Chalmers disagreed. Aside from the obvious—war—what else might have been necessary for the American revolutionaries to achieve the vision Paine outlined?

6. If you were a British colonist in 1776, would you have rebelled against Great Britain? What factors might have shaped your decision?

Thomas Paine, *Common Sense* (1776)[1]

Perhaps the sentiments contained in the following pages, are not *yet* sufficiently fashionable to procure them general favour; a long habit of not thinking a thing *wrong*, gives it a superficial appearance of being *right*, and raises at first a formidable outcry in defense of custom. But the tumult soon subsides. Time makes more converts than reason.

As a long and violent abuse of power, is generally the Means of calling the right of it in question (and in Matters too which might never have been thought of, had not the Sufferers been aggravated into the inquiry) and as the King of England hath undertaken in his *own right*, to support the Parliament in what he calls *Theirs*, and as the good people of this country are grievously oppressed by the combination, they have an undoubted privilege to inquire into the pretensions of both, and equally to reject the usurpation of *either*.

In the following sheets, the author hath studiously avoided every thing which is personal among ourselves. Compliments as well as censure to individuals make no part thereof. The wise, and the worthy, need not the triumph of a pamphlet; and those whose sentiments are injudicious, or unfriendly, will cease of themselves unless too much pains are bestowed upon their conversion.

The cause of America is in a great measure the cause of all mankind. Many circumstances hath, and will arise, which are not local, but universal, and through which the principles of all Lovers of Mankind are affected, and in the Event of which, their Affections are interested. The laying a Country desolate with Fire and Sword, declaring War against the natural rights of all Mankind, and extirpating the Defenders thereof from the Face of the Earth, is the Concern of every Man to whom Nature hath given the Power of feeling ...

OF MONARCHY AND HEREDITARY SUCCESSION

MANKIND being originally equals in the order of creation, the equality could only be destroyed by some subsequent circumstance; the distinctions of rich and poor may in a great measure be accounted for, and that without having recourse to the harsh ill-sounding names of oppression and avarice. Oppression is often the *consequence*, but seldom or never the *means* of riches; and though avarice will preserve a man from being necessitously poor, it generally makes him too timorous to be wealthy.

But there is another and great distinction for which no truly natural or religious reason can be assigned, and that is the distinction of men into KINGS and SUBJECTS. Male and female are the distinctions of nature, good and bad the distinctions of Heaven; but how a race of men came into the world so exalted above the rest, and distinguished like some new species, is worth enquiring into, and whether they are the means of happiness or of misery to mankind. ...

---

1   From Moncure Daniel Conway, ed., *The Writings of Thomas Paine*, Vol 1 [1774–1779] (New York: G.P. Putnam's Sons, 1894), 67–68, 75–76, 79, 81, 84–89, 91, 99–101.

To the evil of monarchy we have added that of hereditary succession; and as the first is a degradation and lessening of ourselves, so the second, claimed as a matter of right, is an insult and an imposition on posterity. For all men being originally equals, *no one* by *birth* could have a right to set up his own family in perpetual preference to all others for ever, and though himself might deserve some decent degree of honors of his contemporaries, yet his descendants might be far too unworthy to inherit them. One of the strongest natural proofs of the folly of hereditary right in kings, is, that nature disapproves it, otherwise she would not so frequently turn it into ridicule, by giving mankind an *ass for a lion*. ...

As to usurpation, no man will be so hardy as to defend it; and that William the Conqueror was an usurper is a fact not to be contradicted. The plain truth is, that the antiquity of English monarchy will not bear looking into.

THOUGHTS ON THE PRESENT STATE OF AMERICAN AFFAIRS

In the following pages I offer nothing more than simple facts, plain arguments, and common sense; and have no other preliminaries to settle with the reader, than that he will divest himself of prejudice and prepossession, and suffer his reason and his feelings to determine for themselves; that he will put on, or rather that he will not put off, the true character of a man, and generously enlarge his views beyond the present day.

Volumes have been written on the subject of the struggle between England and America. Men of all ranks have embarked in the controversy, from different motives, and with various designs; but all have been ineffectual, and the period of debate is closed. Arms, as the last resource, decide the contest; the appeal was the choice of the king, and the continent hath accepted the challenge. ...

The sun never shined on a cause of greater worth. 'Tis not the affair of a city, a county, a province, or a kingdom, but of a continent—of at least one eighth part of the habitable globe. 'Tis not the concern of a day, a year, or an age; posterity are virtually involved in the contest, and will be more or less affected even to the end of time, by the proceedings now. Now is the seed time of continental union, faith and honor. The least fracture now will be like a name engraved with the point of a pin on the tender rind of a young oak; the wound would enlarge with the tree, and posterity read in it full grown characters. ...

As much hath been said of the advantages of reconciliation, which, like an agreeable dream, hath passed away and left us as we were, it is but right that we should examine the contrary side of the argument, and inquire into some of the many material injuries which these colonies sustain, and always will sustain, by being connected with and dependent on Great Britain. To examine that connection and dependence, on the principles of nature and common sense, to see what we have to trust to, if separated, and what we are to expect, if dependent.

I have heard it asserted by some, that as America has flourished under her former connection with Great Britain, the same connection is necessary towards her future happiness, and will always have the same effect. Nothing can be more fallacious than this kind of argument. We may as well assert that because a child has thrived upon milk, that it is never to have meat, or that the first twenty years of our lives is to become a precedent for the next twenty. But even this is admitting more than is true, for I answer roundly that America would have flourished as much, and probably much more, had no European power taken any notice of her. The commerce, by which she hath enriched herself are the necessaries of life, and will always have a market while eating is the custom of Europe.

But she has protected us, say some. That she hath engrossed us is true, and defended the continent at our expense as well as her own, is admitted, and she would have defended Turkey from the same motive, viz. the sake of trade and dominion.

Alas, we have been long led away by ancient prejudices and made large sacrifices to superstition. We have boasted the protection of Great Britain, without considering, that her motive was *interest* not *attachment*; that she did not protect us from *our enemies* on *our account*; but from *her enemies* on *her own account*, from those who had no quarrel with us on any *other account*, and who will always be our enemies on the *same account*. Let Britain waive her pretensions to the continent, or the continent throw off the dependence, and we should be at peace with France and Spain, were they at war with Britain. ...

But Britain is the parent country, say some. Then the more shame upon her conduct. Even brutes do not devour their young, nor savages make war upon their families; wherefore, the assertion, if true, turns to her reproach; but it happens not to be true, or only partly so, and the phrase *parent* or *mother country* hath been jesuitically adopted by the king and his parasites, with a low papistical design of gaining an unfair bias on the credulous weakness of our minds. Europe, and not England, is the parent country of America. This new world hath been the asylum for the persecuted lovers of civil and religious liberty from *every part* of Europe. Hither have they fled, not from the tender embraces of the mother, but from the cruelty of the monster; and it is so far true of England, that the same tyranny which drove the first emigrants from home, pursues their descendants still. ...

Our plan is commerce, and that, well attended to, will secure us the peace and friendship of all Europe; because it is the interest of all Europe to have America a *free port*. Her trade will always be a protection, and her barrenness of gold and silver secure her from invaders.

I challenge the warmest advocate for reconciliation, to shew, a single advantage that this continent can reap by being connected with Great Britain. I repeat the challenge, not a single advantage is derived. Our corn will fetch its price in any market in Europe, and our imported goods must be paid for buy them where we will.

But the injuries and disadvantages which we sustain by that connection, are without number; and our duty to mankind at large, as well as to ourselves, instruct us to renounce the alliance: because, any submission to, or dependence on Great Britain, tends directly to involve this continent in European wars and quarrels; and set us at variance with nations who would otherwise seek our friendship, and against whom we have neither anger nor complaint. As Europe is our market for trade, we ought to form no partial connection with any part of it. It is the true interest of America to steer clear of European contentions, which she never can do, while by her dependence on Britain, she is made the makeweight in the scale of British politics. ...

It is repugnant to reason, to the universal order of things to all examples from former ages, to suppose, that this continent can longer remain subject to any external power. The most sanguine in Britain does not think so. The utmost stretch of human wisdom cannot, at this time, compass a plan short of separation, which can promise the continent even a year's security. Reconciliation is *now* a fallacious dream. Nature hath deserted the connection, and Art cannot supply her place. For, as Milton wisely expresses, "never can true reconcilement grow where wounds of deadly hate have pierced so deep." ...

A government of our own is our natural right: And when a man seriously reflects on the precariousness of human affairs, he will become convinced, that it is infinitely wiser and safer, to form a constitution of our own in a cool deliberate manner, while we have it in our power, than to trust such an interesting event to time and chance. ...

O ye that love mankind! Ye that dare oppose, not only the tyranny, but the tyrant, stand forth! Every spot of the old world is overrun with oppression. Freedom hath been hunted round the globe. Asia, and Africa, have long expelled her. Europe regards her like a stranger, and England hath given her warning to depart. O! receive the fugitive, and prepare in time an asylum for mankind.

James Chalmers, *Plain Truth: Addressed to the Inhabitants of America* (1776)[2]

If, indignant at the doctrine contained in the pamphlet entitled *Common Sense*, I have expressed myself, in the following observations, with some ardor; I entreat the reader to impute my indignation, to honest zeal against the author's insidious tenets. Animated and impelled by every inducement of the human heart, I love, and (if I dare so express myself,) I adore my country. Passionately devoted to true liberty, I glow with the purest flame of patriotism. Silver'd with age as I am, if I know myself, my humble sword shall not be wanting to my country (if the most honorable terms are not tendered by the British nation); to whose sacred cause I am most fervently devoted. The judicious reader will not impute my honest, though bold remarks, to unfriendly designs against my children—against my country; but to abhorrence of independency, which, if effected, would inevitably plunge our once preeminently envied country into ruin, horror, and desolation.

I have now before me the pamphlet intitled Common Sense; on which I shall remark with freedom and candour. ...

Our political quack [tries] to cajole the people into the most abject slavery under the delusive name of independence. His first indecent attack is against the English constitution; which with all its imperfections is, and ever will be the pride and envy of mankind. ... This beautiful system ... our constitution is a compound of monarchy, aristocracy, and democracy. ... Were I asked marks of the best government ... I would reply, the increase, preservation, and prosperity of its members, in no quarter of the globe are those marks so certainly to be found, as in Great Britain, and her dependencies. ...

After his terrible anathema against our venerable constitution and monarchy, let us briefly examine a democratical state; and see whether or not it is a government less sanguinary. This government is extremely plausible, and indeed flattering to the pride of mankind. The demagogues, therefore, to seduce the people into their criminal designs, ever hold up democracy to them; although conscious it never did, nor ever will answer in practice. If we believe a great author, "there never existed, nor ever will exist a real democracy in the world." If we examine the republics of Greece and Rome, we ever find them in a state of war domestic or foreign. Our author therefore makes no mention of these ancient States ...

Can a reasonable being for a moment believe that Great Britain, whose political existence depends on our constitutional obedience, who but yesterday made such prodigious efforts to save us from France, will not exert herself as powerfully to preserve us from our frantic schemes of independency? ... We remember with unfeigned gratitude the many benefits derived through our connections with Great Britain, by whom but yesterday we were emancipated from slavery

---

2   From James Chalmers, *Plain Truth: Addressed to the Inhabitants of America* (Philadelphia: M. Mills, 1776), iii, 1, 2, 5, 15–17, 32, 34.

and death. ... We venerate the constitution, which with all its imperfections (too often exaggerated) we apprehend almost approaches as near to perfection as human kind can bear.

[W]e may predict, that his scheme of independency would soon, very soon, give way to a government imposed on us by some Cromwell of our armies ...

A failure of commerce [would] preclude the numerous tribe of planters, farmers and others, from paying their debts ... A war will ensue between the creditors and their debtors, which will eventually end in a general ... abolition of debts ...

Volumes were insufficient to describe the horror, misery, and desolation awaiting the people at large in the Syren form of American independence. In short, I affirm that it would be most excellent policy in those who wish for true liberty, to submit by an advantageous reconciliation to the authority of Great Britain; "to accomplish in the long run, what they cannot do by hypocrisy, fraud, and force in the short one." Independence and slavery are synonymous terms.

CHAPTER 6

The Contagion of Liberty

The consequences of the American Revolution extended far beyond independence. During the 1770s and 1780s, revolutionary ideals such as liberty and equality permeated American society in unanticipated ways. Drawing upon the Revolution's rhetoric, marginalized groups, including religious minorities, enslaved African Americans, and women, demanded greater social and political equality. In their challenge to the king's authority, American revolutionaries had unleashed a widespread reassessment of power within their own communities and families.

The following documents capture diverse Americans' interpretations of this "contagion of liberty." In the first, David Ramsay recalls the creation of state constitutions after 1776. Ramsay was an elite member of the Revolutionary generation. Trained at what later became Princeton University, he studied medicine before serving as a delegate to the Continental Congress. In his *History of the United States* (1816), Ramsay identified the creation of state constitutions as his country's greatest contribution to the science of government.

Next, a series of petitions by African Americans demonstrate the Revolution's challenge to slavery. Opposition to slavery had emerged earlier, but the Revolution presented enslaved and free people alike with a common language of liberation and equality. As these petitions suggest, African Americans strategically adopted this rhetoric to criticize slavery and to advocate for their freedom.

Finally, the letters of Abigail and John Adams illustrate the ways revolutionary ideas as well as the experience of war challenged patriarchal authority. In the colonies and Britain, husbands enjoyed legal control over their wives' bodies and property—a power, noted Abigail Adams, not unlike the absolute authority of tyrants. As Abigail Adams suggested to her husband, the Revolution presented an opportunity to expand women's legal and political spheres of influence. John Adams's response to her, and a subsequent letter to James Sullivan, reveal his considerable unease with Abigail's suggestion—as well as with the broader contagion of liberty.

FUNDAMENTALS

1. According to Ramsay, what flaws characterized all forms of government prior to the creation of state constitutions?

2. Which parts of the state constitutions did Ramsay most admire? Why?

3. How did John Adams respond to Abigail's insistence that he "not put such unlimited power in the hands of husbands"?

4. What did John Adams find unsettling about the Revolution?

ANALYSIS AND INTERPRETATION

1. What did the Revolution mean for these writers?

2. What persuasive tactics did the African American petitioners employ? Why might their tactics have changed over time?

3. Based on evidence in Abigail Adams's letters, in what ways did women support the Revolutionary struggle? How might this support have influenced women's understanding of their place within American society?

4. What were the limits of the American Revolution's transformative power? In other words, what did the Revolution not change? What explains those limits?

5. To what extent did John Adams admire democracy?

David Ramsay, *History of the United States* (1816)[1]

The far-famed social compact between the people and their rulers, did not apply to the United States. The sovereignty was in the people. In their sovereign capacity by their representatives, they agreed on forms of government for their own security, and deputed certain individuals as their agents to serve them in public stations agreeably to constitutions, which they prescribed for their conduct.

The world has not hitherto exhibited so fair an opportunity for promoting social happiness. It is hoped for the honor of human nature, that the result will prove the fallacy of those theories, which suppose that mankind are incapable of self-government. The ancients, not knowing the doctrine of representation, were apt in their public meetings to run into confusion, but in America this mode of taking the sense of the people, is so well understood, and so completely reduced to system, that its most populous states are often peaceably convened in an assembly of deputies, not too large for orderly deliberation, and yet representing the whole in equal proportions. These popular branches of legislature are miniature pictures of the community, and from the mode of their election are likely to be influenced by the same interests and feelings with the people whom they represent. As a farther security for their fidelity, they are bound by every law they make for their constituents. The assemblage of these circumstances gives as great a security that laws will be made, and government administered for the good of the people, as can be expected from the imperfection of human institutions.

In this short view of the formation and establishment of the American [state] constitutions, we behold our species in a new situation. In no age before, and in no other country, did man ever possess an election of the kind of government, under which he would choose to live. The constituent parts of the ancient free governments were thrown together by accident. The freedom of modern European governments was, for the most part, obtained by the concessions, or liberality of monarchs, or military leaders. In America alone, reason and liberty concurred in the formation of constitutions. It is true, from the infancy of political knowledge in the United States, there were many defects in their forms of government. But in one thing they were all perfect. They left the people in the power of altering and amending them, whenever they pleased. In this happy peculiarity they placed the science of politics on a footing with the other sciences, by opening it to improvements from experience, and the discoveries of future ages. By means of this power of amending American constitutions, the friends of mankind have fondly hoped that oppression will one day be no more, and that political evil will at least be prevented or restrained with as much certainty, by a proper combination or separation of power, as natural evil is lessened or prevented by the application of the knowledge or ingenuity of man to domestic purposes. No part of the history of ancient or modern Europe can furnish a single fact that militates against this opinion, since in none of its governments have the principles of equal representation and checks been applied, for the preservation of freedom. On these two pivots are suspended the

---

1 From David Ramsay, *History of the United States, From Their First Settlement as English Colonies in 1607, to the Year 1808,* Vol. II (Philadelphia: M. Carey and Son, 1816), 172–174.

liberties of most of the states. Where they are wanting, there can be no security for liberty: where they exist, they render any further security unnecessary.

From history the citizens of the United States had been taught, that the maxims, adopted by the rulers of the earth, that society was instituted for the sake of the governors; and that the interests of the many were to be postponed to the convenience of the privileged few, had filled the world with bloodshed and wickedness; while experience had proved, that it is the invariable and natural character of power, whether entrusted or assumed, to exceed its proper limits, and, if unrestrained, to divide the world into masters and slaves. They therefore began upon the opposite maxims, that society was instituted, not for the governors, but the governed; that the interest of the few, should, in all cases, give way to that of the many; that exclusive and hereditary privileges were useless and dangerous institutions in society; and that entrusted authorities should be liable to frequent and periodical recalls. With them the sovereignty of the people was more than a mere theory. The characteristic of that sovereignty was displayed by their authority in written constitutions.

Petitions by African Americans in
New England (1773–1780)[2]

Province of the Massachusetts Bay.

To His Excellency Thomas Hutchinson, Esq., Governor:—

To the Honorable, His Majesty's Council, and To the Honorable House of Representatives in general court assembled at Boston, the 6th day of January, 1773:—The humble petition of many slaves, living in the town of Boston, and other towns in the province is this, namely:—

That your Excellency and Honors, and the Honorable the Representatives, would be pleased to take their unhappy state and condition under your wise and just consideration.

We desire to bless God, who loves mankind, who sent his Son to die for their salvation, and who is no respecter of persons; that he hath lately put it into the hearts of multitudes on both sides of the water, to bear our burthens, some of whom are men of great note and influence; who have pleaded our cause with arguments which we hope will have their weight with this Honorable Court.

We presume not to dictate to Your Excellency and Honors, being willing to rest our cause on your humanity and justice; yet would beg leave to say a word or two on the subject.

Although some of the negroes are vicious (who doubtless may be punished and restrained by the same laws which are in force against other of the King's subjects), there are many others of a quite different character, and who, if made free, would soon be able as well as willing to bear a part in the public charges. Many of them, of good natural parts, are discreet, sober, honest, and industrious; and may it not be said of many, that they are virtuous and religious, although their condition is in itself so unfriendly to religion, and every moral virtue except *patience?* How many of that number have there been, and now are in this province, who have had every day of their lives embittered with this most intolerable reflection, that, let their behavior be what it will, neither they, nor their children, to all generations, shall ever be able to do, or to possess and enjoy any thing—no, not even *life itself*—but in a manner as the *beasts* that perish.

We have no property! we have no wives! we have no children! we have no city! no country! But we have a Father in heaven, and we are determined, as far as his grace shall enable us, and as far as our degraded contemptuous life will admit, to keep all his commandments; especially will we be obedient to our masters, so long as God, in his sovereign providence shall *suffer* us to be holden in bondage.

It would be impudent, if not presumptuous in us, to suggest to Your Excellency and Honors any law or laws proper to be made, in relation to our unhappy state, which, although our greatest

---

2   From Wm. C. Nell, *The Colored Patriots of the American Revolution* (Boston: Robert F. Wallcut, 1855), 40–41, 47–48, 87–88.

unhappiness, is not our *fault*; and this gives us great encouragement to pray and hope for such relief as is consistent with your wisdom, justice and goodness.

We think ourselves very happy, that we may thus address the great and general court of this province, which great and good court is to us, the best judge, under God, of what is wise, just and good.

We humbly beg leave to add but this one thing more: we pray for such relief only, which by no possibility can ever be productive of the least wrong or injury to our masters, but to us will be as life from the dead.

<p style="text-align:center">~~~~~</p>

SECOND PETITION OF MASSACHUSETTS SLAVES.

The petition of a great number of negroes, who are detained in a state of slavery in the very bowels of a free and Christian country, humbly showing,—

That your petitioners apprehend that they have, in common with all other men, a natural and inalienable right to that freedom, which the great Parent of the universe hath bestowed equally on all mankind, and which they have never forfeited by any compact or agreement whatever. But they were unjustly dragged by the cruel hand of power from their dearest friends, and some of them even torn from the embraces of their tender parents,—from a populous, pleasant and plentiful country, and in violation of the laws of nature and nations, and in defiance of all the tender feelings of humanity, brought hither to be sold like beasts of burthen, and, like them, condemned to slavery for life—among a people possessing the mild religion of Jesus—a people not insensible of the sweets of national freedom, nor without a spirit to resent the unjust endeavors of others to reduce them to a state of bondage and subjection.

Your Honors need not to be informed that a life of slavery like that of your petitioners, deprived of every social privilege, of every thing requisite to render life even tolerable, is far worse than nonexistence.

In imitation of the laudable example of the good people of these States, your petitioners have long and patiently waited the event of petition after petition, by them presented to the legislative body of this State, and cannot but with grief reflect that their success has been but too similar.

They cannot but express their astonishment that it has never been considered, that every principle from which America has acted, in the course of her unhappy difficulties with Great Britain, bears stronger than a thousand arguments in favor of your humble petitioners. They therefore humbly beseech Your Honors to give their petition its due weight and consideration, and cause an act of the legislature to be passed, whereby they may be restored to the enjoyment of that freedom, which is the natural right of all men, and their children (who were born in this land of liberty) may not be held as slaves after they arrive at the age of twenty-one years. So may the inhabitants of this State (no longer chargeable with the inconsistency of acting themselves the part which they condemn and oppose in others) be prospered in their glorious struggles for liberty, and have those blessings secured to them by Heaven, of which benevolent minds cannot wish to deprive their fellow-men.

And your petitioners, as in duty bound, shall ever pray:—

> LANCASTER HILL,
> PETER BESS,
> BRISTER SLENFEN,
> PRINCE HALL,
> JACK PIERPONT, [his X mark.]
> NERO FUNELO, [his X mark.]
> NEWPORT SUMNER, [his X mark.]

~~~~~

To the Honorable Council and House of Representatives, in General Court assembled, for the State of the Massachusetts Bay, in New England:

The petition of several poor negroes and mulattoes, who are inhabitants of the town of Dartmouth, humbly showeth,—

That we being chiefly of the African extract, and by reason of long bondage and hard slavery, we have been deprived of enjoying the profits of our labor or the advantage of inheriting estates from our parents, as our neighbors the white people do, having some of us not long enjoyed our own freedom; yet of late, contrary to the invariable custom and practice of the country, we have been, and now are, taxed both in our polls and that small pittance of estate which, through much hard labor and industry, we have got together to sustain ourselves and families withall. We apprehend it, therefore, to be hard usage, and will doubtless (if continued) reduce us to a state of beggary, whereby we shall become a burthen to others, if not timely prevented by the interposition of your justice and power.

Your petitions further show, that we apprehend ourselves to be aggrieved, in that, while we are not allowed the privilege of freemen of the State, having no vote or influence in the election of those that tax us, yet many of our colour (as is well known) have cheerfully entered the field of battle in the defence of the common cause, and that (as we conceive) against a similar exertion of power (in regard to taxation), too well known to need a recital in this place.

We most humbly request, therefore, that you would take our unhappy case into your serious consideration, and, in your wisdom and power, grant us relief from taxation, while under our present depressed circumstances; and your poor petitioners, as in duty bound, shall ever pray, &c.

JOHN CUFFE,
ADVENTUR CHILD,
PAUL CUFFE,
SAMUEL GRAY, X his mark.
PERO HOWARD, X his mark
PERO RUSSELL, X his mark.
PERO COGGESHALL.

Dated at Dartmouth, the 10th of February, 1780

Correspondence of Abigail and John Adams (1776)[3]

ABIGAIL ADAMS TO JOHN ADAMS 31 MARCH, 1776

I wish you would ever write me a letter half as long as I write you, and tell me, if you may, where your fleet are gone; what sort of defense Virginia can make against our common enemy; whether it is so situated as to make an able defense. Are not the gentry lords, and the common people vassals? Are they not like the uncivilized vassals Britain represents us to be? I hope their riflemen, who have shown themselves very savage and even blood-thirsty, are not a specimen of the generality of the people. I am willing to allow the colony great merit for having produced a Washington; but they have been shamefully duped by a Dunmore.

I have sometimes been ready to think that the passion for liberty cannot be equally strong in the breast of those who have been accustomed to deprive their fellow-creatures of theirs. Of this I am certain, that it is not founded upon that generous and Christian principle of doing to others as we would that others should do unto us.

Do not you want to see Boston? I am fearful of the small-pox; or I should have been in before this time. I got Mr. Crane to go to our house and see what a state it was in. I find it has been occupied by one of the doctors of a regiment; very dirty, but no other damage has been done to it. The few things which were left in it are all gone. I look upon it as a new acquisition of property—a property which one month ago I did not value at a single shilling, and would with pleasure have seen it in flames.

The town in general is left in a better state than we expected; more owing to a precipitate flight than any regard to the inhabitants; though some individuals discovered a sense of honor and justice, and have left the rent of the houses in which they were, for the owners, and the furniture unhurt, or, if damaged, sufficient to make it good. Others have committed abominable ravages. The mansion house of your President is safe, and the furniture unhurt; while the house and furniture of the Solicitor General have fallen a prey to their own merciless party. Surely the very friends feel a reverential awe for virtue and patriotism, whilst they detest the parricide and traitor.

I feel very differently at the approach of spring from what I did a month ago. We knew not then whether we could plant or sow with safety, whether where we had tilled we could reap the fruits of our own industry, whether we could rest in our own cottages or whether we should be driven from the seacoast to seek shelter in the wilderness; but now we feel a temporary peace, and the poor fugitives are returning to their deserted habitation.

Though we felicitate ourselves, we sympathize with those who are trembling lest the lot of Boston should be theirs. But they cannot be in similar circumstances unless pusillanimity and

---

3   From Samuel Eliot, ed., *Selections from American Authors* (New York: Taintor Bros., Merrill & Co., 1879), 81–83, 87–88; Charles Francis Adams, ed., *Letters of John Adams, Addressed to His Wife*, Vol. I (Boston: Phillips & Sampson, 1841), 94–97; Charles Francis Adams, ed., *The Works of John Adams, Second President of the United States*, Vol. IX (Boston: Phillips & Sampson, 1854), 375–378.

cowardice should take possession of them. They have time and warning given them to see the evil and shun it.

I long to hear that you have declared an independency. And, by the way, in the new code of laws which I suppose it will be necessary for you to make, I desire you would remember the ladies and be more generous and favorable to them than your ancestors. Do not put such unlimited power into the hands of the husbands. Remember, all men would be tyrants if they could. If particular care and attention is not paid to the ladies, we are determined to foment a rebellion, and will not hold ourselves bound by any laws in which we have no voice or representation.

That your sex are naturally tyrannical is a truth so thoroughly established as to admit of no dispute; but such of you as wish to be happy willingly give up the harsh title of master for the more tender and endearing one of friend. Why, then, not put it out of the power of the vicious and the lawless to use us with cruelty and indignity with impunity? Men of sense in all ages abhor these customs which treat us only as the vassals of your sex; regard us then as beings placed by Providence under your protection, and in imitation of the Supreme Being make use of that power only for our happiness.

JOHN ADAMS TO ABIGAIL ADAMS 14 APRIL, 1776

You justly complain of my short letters, but the critical state of things and the multiplicity of avocations must plead my excuse. You ask where the fleet is? The inclosed papers will inform you. You ask what sort of defense Virginia can make? I believe they will make an able defense. Their militia and minute-men have been some time employed in training themselves, and they have nine battalions of regulars, as they call them, maintained among them, under good officers, at the Continental expense. They have set up a number of manufactories of firearms, which are busily employed. They are tolerably supplied with powder, and are successful and assiduous in making saltpetre. Their neighboring sister, or rather daughter colony of North Carolina, which is a warlike colony, and has several battalions at the Continental expense, as well as a pretty good militia, are ready to assist them, and they are in very good spirits and seem determined to make a brave resistance. The gentry are very rich, and the common people very poor. This inequality of property gives an aristocratical turn to all their proceedings, and occasions a strong aversion in their patricians to "Common Sense." But the spirit of these barons is coming down, and it must submit. It is very true, as you observe, they have been duped by Dunmore. But this is a common case. All the colonies are duped, more or less, at one time and another. A more egregious bubble was never blown up than the story of Commissioners coming to treat with the Congress, yet it has gained credit like a charm, not only with, but against the clearest evidence. I never shall forget the delusion which seized our best and most sagacious friends, the dear inhabitants of Boston, the winter before last. Credulity and the want of foresight are imperfections in the human character, that no politician can sufficiently guard against.

You give me some pleasure by your account of a certain house in Queen Street. I had burned it long ago in imagination. It rises now to my view like a phoenix. What shall I say of the Solicitor General? I pity his pretty children. I pity his father and his sisters. I wish I could be clear that it is no moral evil to pity him and his lady. Upon repentance, they will certainly have a large share in the compassions of many. But let us take warning, and give it to our children. Whenever vanity and gayety, a love of pomp and dress, furniture, equipage, buildings, great company, expensive diversions, and elegant entertainments get the better of the principles and judgments of men or women, there is no knowing where they will stop, nor into what evils, natural, moral, or political, they will lead us.

Your description of your own *gaité de coeur* charms me. Thanks be to God, you have just cause to rejoice, and may the bright prospect be obscured by no cloud. As to declarations of independency, be patient. Read our privateering laws and our commercial laws. What signifies a word?

As to your extraordinary code of laws, I cannot but laugh. We have been told that our struggle has loosened the bonds of government everywhere; that children and apprentices were disobedient; that schools and colleges were grown turbulent; that Indians slighted their guardians, and negroes grew insolent to their masters. But your letter was the first intimation that another tribe, more numerous and powerful than all the rest, were grown discontented. This is rather too coarse a compliment, but you are so saucy, I won't blot it out. Depend upon it, we know better than to repeal our masculine systems. Although they are in full force, you know they are little more than theory. We dare not exert our power in its full latitude. We are obliged to go fair and softly, and, in practice, you know we are the subjects. We have only the name of masters, and rather than give up this, which would completely subject us to the despotism of the petticoat, I hope General Washington and all our brave heroes would fight; I am sure every good politician would plot, as long as he would against despotism, empire, monarchy, aristocracy, oligarchy, or ochlocracy. A fine story, indeed! I begin to think the ministry as deep as they are wicked. After stirring up Tories, land-jobbers, trimmers, bigots, Canadians, Indians, negroes, Hanoverians, Hessians, Russians, Irish Roman Catholics, Scotch renegadoes, at last they have stimulated the ladies to demand new privileges and threaten to rebel.

ABIGAIL ADAMS TO JOHN ADAMS 7 MAY, 1776

How many are the solitary hours I spend ruminating upon the past and anticipating the future, whilst you, overwhelmed with the cares of state, have but a few moments you can devote to any individual. All domestic pleasures and enjoyments are absorbed in the great and important duty you owe your country, "for our country is, as it were, a secondary god, and the first and greatest parent. It is to be preferred to wives, parents, children, friends, and all things,—the gods only excepted; for, if our country perishes, it is as impossible to save an individual as to preserve one of the fingers of the mortified hand." Thus do I suppress every wish, and silence every murmur, acquiescing in a painful separation from the companion of my youth and the friend of my heart.

I believe 't is near ten days since I wrote you a line. I have not felt in a humor to entertain you. If I had taken up my pen perhaps some unbecoming invective might have fallen from it. The eyes of our rulers have been closed, and a lethargy has seized almost every member. I fear a fatal security has taken possession of them. Whilst the building is in flames, they tremble at the expense of water to quench it. In short, two months have elapsed since the evacuation of Boston, and very little has been done in that time to secure it, or the harbor, from future invasion. The people are all in a flame, and no one among us, that I have heard of, even mentions expense. They think, universally, that there has been an amazing neglect somewhere. Many have turned out as volunteers to work upon Noddle's island, and many more would go upon Nantasket, if the business was once set on foot. " 'T is a maxim of state, that power and liberty are like heat and moisture. Where they are well mixed, everything prospers; where they are single, they are destructive."

A government of more stability is much wanted in this colony, and they are ready to receive it from the hands of the Congress. And since I have begun with maxims of state, I will add another, namely, that a people may let a king fall, yet still remain a people; but, if a king let his people slip from him, he is no longer a king. And as this is most certainly our case, why not proclaim to the world, in decisive terms, your own importance?

Shall we not be despised by foreign powers, for hesitating so long at a word?

I cannot say that I think you are very generous to the ladies; for, whilst you are proclaiming peace and good-will to men, emancipating all nations, you insist upon retaining an absolute power over wives. But you must remember that arbitrary power is like most other things which are very hard, very liable to be broken; and, notwithstanding all your wise laws and maxims, we have it in our power, not only to free ourselves, but to subdue our masters, and, without violence, throw both your natural and legal authority at our feet;—

> *"Charm by accepting, by submitting sway,*
> *Yet have our humor most when we obey."*

I thank you for several letters which I have received since I wrote last; they alleviate a tedious absence, and I long earnestly for a Saturday evening, and experience a similar pleasure to that which I used to find in the return of my friend upon that day after a week's absence. The idea of a year dissolves all my philosophy.

Our little ones, whom you so often recommend to my care and instruction, shall not be deficient in virtue or probity, if the precepts of a mother have their desired effect; but they would be doubly enforced, could they be indulged with the example of a father alternately before them. I often point them to their sire,—

> *"engaged in a corrupted state,*
> *Wrestling with vice and faction."*

JOHN ADAMS TO JAMES SULLIVAN 26 MAY, 1776

Your favors of May 9th and 17th are now before me; and I consider them as the commencement of a correspondence which will not only give me pleasure, but may be of service to the public, as in my present station I stand in need of the best intelligence, and the advice of every gentleman of abilities and public principles in the colonies which has seen fit to place me here.

Our worthy friend, Mr. Gerry, has put into my hands a letter from you, of the sixth of May, in which you consider the principles of representation and legislation, and give us hints of some alterations, which you seem to think necessary, in the qualification of voters.

I wish, Sir, I could possibly find time to accompany you, in your investigation of the principles upon which a representative assembly stands, and ought to stand, and in your examination, whether the practice of our colony has been conformable to those principles. But, alas! Sir, my time is so incessantly engrossed by the business before me, that I cannot spare enough to go through so large a field; and as to books, it is not easy to obtain them here; nor could I find a moment to look into them, if I had them.

It is certain, in theory, that the only moral foundation of government is, the consent of the people. But to what an extent shall we carry this principle? Shall we say that every individual of the community, old and young, male and female, as well as rich and poor, must consent, expressly, to every act of legislation? No, you will say, this is impossible. How, then, does the right arise in the majority to govern the minority, against their will? Whence arises the right of the men to govern the women, without their consent? Whence the right of the old to bind the young, without theirs?

But let us first suppose that the whole community, of every rank, age, sex, and condition, has a right to vote. This community is assembled. A motion is made, and carried by a majority of one voice. The minority will not agree to this. Whence arise the right of the majority to govern, and the obligation of the minority to obey?

From necessity, you will say, because there can be no other rule.

But why exclude women?

You will say, because their delicacy renders them unfit for practice and experience in the great businesses of life, and the hardy enterprises of war, as well as the arduous cares of state. Besides, their attention is so much engaged with the necessary nurture of their children, that nature has made them fittest for domestic cares. And children have not judgment or will of their own. True. But will not these reasons apply to others? Is it not equally true, that men in general, in every society, who are wholly destitute of property, are also too little acquainted with public affairs to form a right judgment, and too dependent upon other men to have a will of their own? If this is a fact, if you give to every man who has no property, a vote, will you not make a fine encouraging provision for corruption, by your fundamental law? Such is the frailty of the human heart, that very few men that have no property, have any judgment of their own. They talk and vote as they are directed by some man of property, who has attached their minds to his interest.

Upon my word, Sir, I have long thought an army a piece of clock-work, and to be governed only by principles and maxims, as fixed as any in mechanics; and, by all that I have read in the history of mankind, and in authors who have speculated upon society and government, I am much inclined to think a government must manage a society in the same manner; and that this is machinery too.

Harrington has shown that power always follows property. This I believe to be as infallible a maxim in politics, as that action and reaction are equal, is in mechanics. Nay, I believe we may advance one step farther, and affirm that the balance of power in a society, accompanies the balance of property in a land. The only possible way then, of preserving the balance of power on the side of equal liberty and public virtue, is to make the acquisition of land easy to every member of society; to make a division of the land into small quantities, so that the multitude may be possessed of landed estates. If the multitude is possessed of the balance of real estate, the multitude will have the balance of power, and in that case the multitude will take care of liberty, virtue, and the interest of the multitude, in all acts of government.

I believe these principles have been felt, if not understood, in the Massachusetts Bay, from the beginning; and therefore I should think that wisdom and policy would dictate in these times to be very cautious of making alterations. Our people have never been very rigid in scrutinizing into the qualifications of voters, and I presume they will not now begin to be so. But I would not advise them to make any alteration in the laws, at present, respecting the qualifications of voters.

Your idea that those laws which affect the lives and personal liberty of all, or which inflict corporal punishment, affect those who are not qualified to vote, as well as those who are, is just. But so they do women, as well as men; children, as well as adults. What reason should there be for excluding a man of twenty years eleven months and twenty-seven days old, from a vote, when you admit one who is twenty-one? The reason is you must fix upon some period in life, when the understanding and will of men in general, is fit to be trusted by the public. Will not the same reason justify in fixing upon some certain quality of property, as a qualification?

The same reasoning which will induce you to admit all men who have no property, to vote, with those who have, for those laws which affect the person, will prove that you ought to admit women and children; for, generally speaking, women and children have as good judgments, and as independent minds, as those men who are wholly destitute of property, these last being to all intents and purposes as much dependent upon others, who will please to feed, clothe, and employ them, as women are upon their husbands, or children on their parents.

As to your idea of proportioning the votes of men, in money matters, to the property they hold, it is utterly impracticable. There is no possible way of ascertaining, at any one time, how much every man in the community is worth; and if there was, so fluctuating is trade and property, that this state of it would change in half an hour. The property of the whole community is shifting every hour, and no record can be kept of the changes.

Society can be governed only by general rules. Government cannot accommodate itself to every particular case as it happens, nor to circumstances of particular persons. It must establish general comprehensive regulations for cases and persons. The only question is, which general rule will accommodate most cases and most persons.

Depend upon it, Sir, it is dangerous to open so fruitful a source of controversy and altercation as would be opened by attempting to alter the qualifications of voters; there will be no end of it. New claims will arise; women will demand a vote; lads from twelve to twenty-one will think their rights not enough attended to; and every man who has not a farthing, will demand an equal voice with any other, in all acts of state. It tends to confound and destroy all distinctions, and prostrate all ranks to one common level.

CHAPTER 7

Creating the Constitution, Revising the Revolution

The United States Constitution was a product of the chaotic political and economic climate of the 1780s. One of the primary causes of this chaos was the deep economic depression that struck the new nation after independence. During the war, farmers and artisans had borrowed heavily, and with the onset of the postwar depression, many of these debtors became unable to repay their loans. Faced with financial ruin, both debtors and creditors petitioned their states for relief. No matter what policies state governments pursued, controversy followed. When states supported debtors by printing paper money or reducing taxes, creditors complained that their property rights—in this case, the repayment of their loans—had been violated. When states supported creditors by raising taxes or punishing delinquent borrowers, debtors violently defended their endangered homes and farms. Tensions exploded in 1786 with Shays's Rebellion, when indebted Massachusetts farmers attempted to seize the state government before being put down by a state-backed militia. Meanwhile, Congress lacked authority under the Articles of Confederation to resolve these issues.

The delegates who convened at the Philadelphia Convention in 1787 sought to address the economic and political crises of the 1780s. The document they produced—the United States Constitution—incited intense controversy and heated debate. Supporters of the Constitution became known as "Federalists," while opponents became known as "Antifederalists."

Below are two classic examples of Federalist and Antifederalist writings. James Madison, one of the Constitution's primary authors, published "Federalist 10" in the months after the convention as he, John Jay, and Alexander Hamilton made the case for ratification in newspapers. Mercy Otis Warren, an educated woman from an elite Massachusetts family (who published under a pseudonym), encapsulated the Antifederalist position with her "Observations on the New Constitution."

FUNDAMENTALS

1. What did James Madison mean by "faction"? What caused factions to develop?

2. Why did Madison think factions presented a problem for popular government?

3. How did Madison think that the "extended republic" created by the U.S. Constitution would remedy the "disease" of faction?

4. What were Mercy Otis Warren's general fears about the U.S. Constitution?

5. Which of Warren's specific (numbered) concerns remind you of complaints lodged against the federal government in the twenty-first century? Which seem less familiar?

ANALYSIS AND INTERPRETATION

1. To what extent did these authors agree about who stood to benefit and who stood to lose if the U.S. Constitution was ratified?

2. Was the U.S. Constitution intended to protect minorities? How so?

3. Warren argued that the framers of the U.S. Constitution thought that "we are incapable of enjoying our liberties—and that we must have a master." Was she accurately portraying Madison's argument? Do you agree with this characterization of human beings?

4. Did the U.S. Constitution represent a continuation of the republican spirit that had previously guided the American Revolution, or did it constitute a departure from that spirit? Put another way, might we describe the U.S. Constitution as counter-revolutionary—as a move away from the fundamental values of the Revolution?

5. To what extent did these writers see the U.S. Constitution as the foundation of an expanding American empire?

James Madison, *Federalist 10*: "The Utility of the Union as a Safeguard Against Domestic Faction and Insurrection" (1787)[1]

AMONG the numerous advantages promised by a well constructed Union, none deserves to be more accurately developed than its tendency to break and control the violence of faction. The friend of popular governments never finds himself so much alarmed for their character and fate, as when he contemplates their propensity to this dangerous vice. He will not fail, therefore, to set a due value on any plan which, without violating the principles to which he is attached, provides a proper cure for it. The instability, injustice, and confusion introduced into the public councils, have, in truth, been the mortal diseases under which popular governments have everywhere perished; as they continue to be the favorite and fruitful topics from which the adversaries to liberty derive their most specious declamations. The valuable improvements made by the American [state] constitutions on the popular models, both ancient and modern, cannot certainly be too much admired; but it would be an unwarrantable partiality, to contend that they have as effectually obviated the danger on this side, as was wished and expected. Complaints are everywhere heard from our most considerate and virtuous citizens, equally the friends of public and private faith, and of public and personal liberty, that our governments are too unstable, that the public good is disregarded in the conflicts of rival parties, and that measures are too often decided, not according to the rules of justice and the rights of the minor party, but by the superior force of an interested and overbearing majority. However anxiously we may wish that these complaints had no foundation, the evidence of known facts will not permit us to deny that they are in some degree true. It will be found, indeed, on a candid review of our situation, that some of the distresses under which we labor have been erroneously charged on the operation of our governments; but it will be found, at the same time, that other causes will not alone account for many of our heaviest misfortunes; and, particularly, for that prevailing and increasing distrust of public engagements, and alarm for private rights, which are echoed from one end of the continent to the other. These must be chiefly, if not wholly, effects of the unsteadiness and injustice with which a factious spirit has tainted our public administrations.

By a faction, I understand a number of citizens, whether amounting to a majority or a minority of the whole, who are united and actuated by some common impulse of passion, or of interest, adverse to the rights of other citizens, or to the permanent and aggregate interests of the community.

There are two methods of curing the mischiefs of faction: the one, by removing its causes; the other, by controlling its effects.

---

1   From Publius, "The Utility of the Union as a Safeguard Against Domestic Faction and Insurrection," *Daily Advertiser* (New York, NY), Nov. 22, 1787.

There are again two methods of removing the causes of faction: the one, by destroying the liberty which is essential to its existence; the other, by giving to every citizen the same opinions, the same passions, and the same interests.

It could never be more truly said than of the first remedy, that it was worse than the disease. Liberty is to faction what air is to fire, an aliment without which it instantly expires. But it could not be less folly to abolish liberty, which is essential to political life, because it nourishes faction, than it would be to wish the annihilation of air, which is essential to animal life, because it imparts to fire its destructive agency.

The second expedient is as impracticable as the first would be unwise. As long as the reason of man continues fallible, and he is at liberty to exercise it, different opinions will be formed. As long as the connection subsists between his reason and his self-love, his opinions and his passions will have a reciprocal influence on each other; and the former will be objects to which the latter will attach themselves. The diversity in the faculties of men, from which the rights of property originate, is not less an insuperable obstacle to a uniformity of interests. The protection of these faculties is the first object of government. From the protection of different and unequal faculties of acquiring property, the possession of different degrees and kinds of property immediately results; and from the influence of these on the sentiments and views of the respective proprietors, ensues a division of the society into different interests and parties.

The latent causes of faction are thus sown in the nature of man; and we see them everywhere brought into different degrees of activity, according to the different circumstances of civil society. A zeal for different opinions concerning religion, concerning government, and many other points, as well of speculation as of practice; an attachment to different leaders ambitiously contending for preeminence and power; or to persons of other descriptions whose fortunes have been interesting to the human passions, have, in turn, divided mankind into parties, inflamed them with mutual animosity, and rendered them much more disposed to vex and oppress each other than to cooperate for their common good. So strong is this propensity of mankind to fall into mutual animosities, that where no substantial occasion presents itself, the most frivolous and fanciful distinctions have been sufficient to kindle their unfriendly passions and excite their most violent conflicts. But the most common and durable source of factions has been the various and unequal distribution of property. Those who hold and those who are without property have ever formed distinct interests in society. Those who are creditors, and those who are debtors, fall under a like discrimination. A landed interest, a manufacturing interest, a mercantile interest, a moneyed interest, with many lesser interests, grow up of necessity in civilized nations, and divide them into different classes, actuated by different sentiments and views. The regulation of these various and interfering interests forms the principal task of modern legislation, and involves the spirit of party and faction in the necessary and ordinary operations of the government.

No man is allowed to be a judge in his own cause, because his interest would certainly bias his judgment, and, not improbably, corrupt his integrity. With equal, nay with greater reason, a body of men are unfit to be both judges and parties at the same time; yet what are many of the most important acts of legislation, but so many judicial determinations, not indeed concerning the rights of single persons, but concerning the rights of large bodies of citizens? And what are the different classes of legislators but advocates and parties to the causes which they determine? Is a law proposed concerning private debts? It is a question to which the creditors are parties on one side and the debtors on the other. Justice ought to hold the balance between them. Yet the parties are, and must be, themselves the judges; and the most numerous party, or, in other words, the most powerful faction must be expected to prevail. Shall domestic manufactures be encouraged, and in what degree, by restrictions on foreign manufactures? are questions which would be differently decided by the landed and the manufacturing classes, and probably by neither with a sole regard to justice and the public good. The apportionment of taxes on the various descriptions of property is an act which seems to require the most exact impartiality; yet there is, perhaps, no legislative act in which greater opportunity and temptation are given to a predominant party to trample on the rules of justice. Every shilling with which they overburden the inferior number, is a shilling saved to their own pockets.

It is in vain to say that enlightened statesmen will be able to adjust these clashing interests, and render them all subservient to the public good. Enlightened statesmen will not always be at the helm. Nor, in many cases, can such an adjustment be made at all without taking into view indirect and remote considerations, which will rarely prevail over the immediate interest which one party may find in disregarding the rights of another or the good of the whole.

The inference to which we are brought, is, that the *causes* of faction cannot be removed; and that relief is only to be sought in the means of controlling its *effects*.

If a faction consists of less than a majority, relief is supplied by the republican principle, which enables the majority to defeat its sinister views by regular vote. It may clog the administration, it may convulse the society; but it will be unable to execute and mask its violence under the forms of the Constitution. When a majority is included in a faction, the form of popular government, on the other hand, enables it to sacrifice to its ruling passion or interest both the public good and the rights of other citizens. To secure the public good and private rights against the danger of such a faction, and at the same time to preserve the spirit and the form of popular government, is then the great object to which our inquiries are directed. Let me add that it is the great desideratum by which this form of government can be rescued from the opprobrium under which it has so long labored, and be recommended to the esteem and adoption of mankind.

By what means is this object attainable? Evidently by one of two only. Either the existence of the same passion or interest in a majority at the same time must be prevented, or the majority, having such coexistent passion or interest, must be rendered, by their number and local situation, unable to concert and carry into effect schemes of oppression. If the impulse and the opportunity be suffered to coincide, we well know that neither moral nor religious motives can be relied on as an adequate control. They are not found to be such on the injustice and violence of individuals, and lose their efficacy in proportion to the number combined together, that is, in proportion as their efficacy becomes needful.

From this view of the subject it may be concluded that a pure democracy, by which I mean a society consisting of a small number of citizens, who assemble and administer the government in person, can admit of no cure for the mischiefs of faction. A common passion or interest will, in almost every case, be felt by a majority of the whole; a communication and concert result from the form of government itself; and there is nothing to check the inducements to sacrifice the weaker party or an obnoxious individual. Hence it is that such democracies have ever been spectacles of turbulence and contention; have ever been found incompatible with personal security or the rights of property; and have in general been as short in their lives as they have been violent in their deaths. Theoretic politicians, who have patronized this species of government, have erroneously supposed that by reducing mankind to a perfect equality in their political rights, they would, at the same time, be perfectly equalized and assimilated in their possessions, their opinions, and their passions.

A republic, by which I mean a government in which the scheme of representation takes place, opens a different prospect, and promises the cure for which we are seeking. Let us examine the points in which it varies from pure democracy, and we shall comprehend both the nature of the cure and the efficacy which it must derive from the Union.

The two great points of difference between a democracy and a republic are: first, the delegation of the government, in the latter, to a small number of citizens elected by the rest; secondly, the greater number of citizens, and greater sphere of country, over which the latter may be extended.

The effect of the first difference is, on the one hand, to refine and enlarge the public views, by passing them through the medium of a chosen body of citizens, whose wisdom may best discern the true interest of their country, and whose patriotism and love of justice will be least likely to sacrifice it to temporary or partial considerations. Under such a regulation, it may well happen that the public voice, pronounced by the representatives of the people, will be more consonant to the public good than if pronounced by the people themselves, convened for the purpose. On the other hand, the effect may be inverted. Men of factious tempers, of local prejudices, or of sinister designs, may, by intrigue, by corruption, or by other means, first obtain the suffrages, and then betray the interests, of the people. The question resulting is, whether small or extensive republics are more favorable to the election of proper guardians of the public weal; and it is clearly decided in favor of the latter by two obvious considerations:

In the first place, it is to be remarked that, however small the republic may be, the representatives must be raised to a certain number, in order to guard against the cabals of a few; and that, however large it may be, they must be limited to a certain number, in order to guard against the confusion of a multitude. Hence, the number of representatives in the two cases not being in proportion to that of the two constituents, and being proportionally greater in the small republic, it follows that, if the proportion of fit characters be not less in the large than in the small republic, the former will present a greater option, and consequently a greater probability of a fit choice.

In the next place, as each representative will be chosen by a greater number of citizens in the large than in the small republic, it will be more difficult for unworthy candidates to practice with success the vicious arts by which elections are too often carried; and the suffrages of the people being more free, will be more likely to centre in men who possess the most attractive merit and the most diffusive and established characters.

It must be confessed that in this, as in most other cases, there is a mean, on both sides of which inconveniences will be found to lie. By enlarging too much the number of electors, you render the representatives too little acquainted with all their local circumstances and lesser interests; as by reducing it too much, you render him unduly attached to these, and too little fit to comprehend and pursue great and national objects. The federal Constitution forms a happy combination in this respect; the great and aggregate interests being referred to the national, the local and particular to the State legislatures.

The other point of difference is, the greater number of citizens and extent of territory which may be brought within the compass of republican than of democratic government; and it is this circumstance principally which renders factious combinations less to be dreaded in the former than in the latter. The smaller the society, the fewer probably will be the distinct parties and interests composing it; the fewer the distinct parties and interests, the more frequently will a majority be found of the same party; and the smaller the number of individuals composing a majority, and the smaller the compass within which they are placed, the more easily will they concert and execute their plans of oppression. Extend the sphere, and you take in a greater variety of parties and interests; you make it less probable that a majority of the whole will have a common motive to invade the rights of other citizens; or if such a common motive exists, it will be more difficult for all who feel it to discover their own strength, and to act in unison with each other. Besides other impediments, it may be remarked that, where there is a consciousness of unjust or dishonorable purposes, communication is always checked by distrust in proportion to the number whose concurrence is necessary.

Hence, it clearly appears, that the same advantage which a republic has over a democracy, in controlling the effects of faction, is enjoyed by a large over a small republic, —is enjoyed by the Union over the States composing it. Does the advantage consist in the substitution of representatives whose enlightened views and virtuous sentiments render them superior to local prejudices and schemes of injustice? It will not be denied that the representation of the Union will be most likely to possess these requisite endowments. Does it consist in the greater security afforded by a greater variety of parties, against the event of any one party being able to outnumber and oppress the rest? In an equal degree does the increased variety of parties comprised within the Union, increase this security. Does it, in fine, consist in the greater obstacles opposed to the concert and accomplishment of the secret wishes of an unjust and interested majority? Here, again, the extent of the Union gives it the most palpable advantage.

The influence of factious leaders may kindle a flame within their particular States, but will be unable to spread a general conflagration through the other States. A religious sect may degenerate into a political faction in a part of the Confederacy; but the variety of sects dispersed over the entire face of it must secure the national councils against any danger from that source. A rage for paper money, for an abolition of debts, for an equal division of property, or for any other improper or wicked project, will be less apt to pervade the whole body of the Union than a particular member of it; in the same proportion as such a malady is more likely to taint a particular county or district, than an entire State.

In the extent and proper structure of the Union, therefore, we behold a republican remedy for the diseases most incident to republican government. And according to the degree of pleasure and pride we feel in being republicans, ought to be our zeal in cherishing the spirit and supporting the character of Federalists.

Mercy Otis Warren, "Observations on the New Constitution" (1788)[2]

Animated with the firmest zeal for the interest of this country, the peace and union of the American States, and the freedom and happiness of a people who have made the most costly sacrifices in the cause of liberty,—who have braved the power of Britain, weathered the convulsions of war, and waded thro' the blood of friends and foes to establish their independence and to support the freedom of the human mind ... obliges every one to remonstrate against the strides of ambition, and a wanton lust of domination, and to resist the first approaches of tyranny, which at this day threaten to sweep away the rights for which the brave Sons of America have fought with an heroism scarcely paralleled even in ancient republicks. ... On these shores freedom has planted her standard, diped in the purple tide that flowed from the veins of her martyred heroes; and here every uncorrupted American yet hopes to see it supported by the vigour, the justice, the wisdom and unanimity of the people, in spite of the deep-laid plots the secret intrigues, or the bold eftrontery of those interested and avricious adventurers for place, who intoxicated with the ideas of distinction and preferment have prostrated every worthy principle beneath the shrine of ambition. Yet these are the men who tell us republicanism is dwindled into theory—that we are incapable of enjoying our liberties—and that we must have a master.— Let us retrospect the days of our adversity, and recollect who were then our friends; do we find them among the sticklers for aristocratick authority? No, they were generally the same men who now wish to save us from the distractions of anarchy on the one hand, and the jaws of tyranny on the other; where then were the class who now come forth importunately urging that our political salvation depends on the adoption of a system at which freedom spurns?—Were not some of them hidden in the corners of obscurity, and others wrapping themselves in the bosom of our enemies for safety? Some of them were in the arms of infancy; and others speculating for fortune, by sporting with public money; while a few, a very few of them were magnanimously defending their country, and raising a character, which I pray heaven may never be sullied by aiding measures derogatory to their former exertions. But the revolutions in principle which time produces among mankind, frequently exhibits the most mortifying instances of human weakness; and this alone can account for the extraordinary appearance of a few names, once distinguished in the honourable walks of patriotism, but now found in the list of the Massachusetts assent to the ratification of a Constitution, which, by the undefined meaning of some parts, and the ambiguities of expression in others, is dangerously adapted to the purposes of an immediate aristocratic tyranny; that from the difficulty, if not impracticability of its operation, must soon terminate in the most uncontrouled despotism.

And it is with inexpressible anxiety, that many of the best friends of the Union of the States—to the peaceable and equal participation of the rights of nature, and to the glory and dignity of

---

2   From A Columbian Patriot, *Observations on the New Constitution, and on the Federal and State Conventions* (Boston: Thomas Greenleaf, 1788), 3–6, 7–9, 10, 11–13, 14, 16, 21, 22.

this country, behold the insiduous arts, and the strenuous efforts of the partisans of arbitrary power, by their vague definitions of the best established truths, endeavoring to envelope the mind in darkness the concomitant of slavery, and to lock the strong chains of domestic despotism on a country, which by the most glorious and successful struggles is but newly emancipated from the spectre of foreign dominion.

I will not expatiate long on a Republican form of government, founded on the principles of monarchy—a democratick branch with the features of artistocracy—and the extravagance of nobility pervading the minds of many of the candidates for office. ... Some gentlemen, with laboured zeal, have spent much time in urging the necessity of government, from the embarrassments of trade—the want of respectability abroad and confidence of the public engagements at home:—These are obvious truths which no one denies; and there are few who do not unite in the general wish for the restoration of public faith, the revival of commerce, arts, agriculture, and industry, under a lenient, peaceable and energetick government: But the most sagacious advocates for the party have not by fair discusion, and rational argumentation, evinced the necessity of adopting this many headed monster; of such motley mixture, that its enemies cannot trace a feature of Democratick or Republican extract; nor have its friends the courage to denominate a Monarchy, an Aristocracy, or an Oligarchy, and the favoured bantling must have passed through the short period of its existence without a name, had not Mr. Wilson, in the fertility of his genius, suggested the happy epithet of a Federal Republic.

It will be allowed by every one that the fundamental principle of a free government is the equal representation of a free people. ... And when society has thus deputed a certain number of their equals to take care of their personal rights, and the interest of the whole community, it must be considered that responsibility is the great security of integrity and honour; and that annual election is the basis of responsibility ... as the best political writers have supported the principles of annual elections with a precision, that cannot be confuted, though they may be darkned, by the sophistical arguments that have been thrown out with design, to undermine all the barriers of freedom.

2. There is no security in the profered system, either for the rights of conscience or the liberty of the Press: Despotism usually while it is gaining ground, will suffer men to think, say, or write what they please; but when once established, if it is thought necessary to subserve the purposes, of arbitrary power, the most unjust restrictions may take place in the first instance, and an *imprimator* on the Press in the next, may silence the complaints, and forbid the most decent remonstrances of an injured and oppressed people.

3. There are no well defined limits of the Judiciary Powers, they seem to be left as a boundless ocean, that has broken over the chart of the Supreme Lawgiver, *"thus far shalt thou go and no further,"* and as they cannot be comprehended by the clearest capacity, or the most sagacious mind, it would be an Herculean labour to attempt to describe the dangers with which they are replete.

4. The Executive and the Legislative are so dangerously blended as to give just cause of alarm, and everything relative thereto, is couched in such ambiguous terms—in such vague and

indefinite expression, as is a sufficient ground without any objection, for the reprobation of a system ...

6. Though it has been said by Mr. *Wilson* and many others, that a Standing-Army is necessary for the dignity and safety of America, yet freedom revolts at the idea, when the ... Despot, may draw out his dragoons to suppress the murmurs of a few, who may yet cherish those sublime principles which call forth the exertions, and lead to the best improvements of the human mind. By the edicts of an authority vested in the sovereign power by the proposed constitution, the militia of the country, the bulwark of defence, and the security of national liberty if no longer under the controul of civil authority; but at the rescript of the Monarch, or the aristocracy, they may either be employed to extort the enormous sums that will be necessary to support the civil list—to maintain the regalia of power—and the splendour of the most useless part of the community, or they may be sent into foreign countries for the fulfilment of treaties, stipulated by the President and two-thirds of the Senate.

7. Notwithstanding the delusory promise to guarantee a Republican form of government to every State in the Union—If the most discerning eye could discover any meaning at all in the engagement, there are no resources left for the support of internal government or the liquidation of the debts of the State. Every source of revenue is in the monopoly of Congress.

8. As the new Congress are empowered to determine their own salaries, the requisitions for this purpose may not be very moderate, and the drain for public moneys will probably rise past all calculation ...

9. There is no provision for a rotation, nor anything to prevent the perpetuity of office in the same hands for life; which by a little well timed bribery, will probably be done, to the exclusion of men of the best abilities from their share in the offices of government.— By this neglect we lose the advantages of that check to the overbearing insolence of office, which by rendering him ineligible at certain periods, keeps the mind of man in equilibrio, and teaches him the feelings of the governed, and better qualifies him to govern in his turn.

10. The inhabitants of the United States, are liable to be dragged from the vicinity of their own country, or state, to answer the litigious or unjust suit of an adversary, on the most distant borders of the Continent: in short the appelate jurisdiction of the Supreme Federal Court, includes an unwarrantable stretch of power over the liberty, life, and property of the subject, through the wide Continent of America.

11. One Representative to thirty thousand inhabitants is a very inadequate representation; and every man who is not lost to all sense of freedom to his country, must reprobate the idea of Congress altering by law, or on any pretence whatever, interfering with any regulations for time, places, and manner of choosing our own Representatives.

12. If the sovereignty of America is designed to be elective, the surcumscribing the votes to only ten electors in this State, and the same proportion in all the others, is nearly tantamount to the exclusion of the voice of the people in the choice of their first magistrate. It is vesting the

choice solely in an aristocratic junto, who may easily combine in each State to place at the head of the Union the most convenient instrument for despotic sway.

13. A Senate chosen for six years will, in most instances, be an appointment for life, as the influence of such a body over the minds of the people will be coequal to the extensive powers with which they are vested, and they will not only forget, but be forgotten by their constituents—a branch of the Supreme Legislature thus set beyond all responsibility is totally repugnant to every principle of a free government.

14. There is no provision by a bill of rights to guard against the dangerous encroachments of power in too many instances to be named ... We are told ... "that the whole constitution is a declaration of rights,"— but mankind must think for themselves, and to many very judicious and discerning characters, the whole constitution with very few exceptions appears a perversion of the rights of particular states, and of private citizens. But the gentleman goes on to tell us, "that the primary object is the general government, and that the rights of individuals are only incidentally mentioned, and that there was a clear impropriety in being very particular about them." ... The rights of individuals ought to be the primary object of all government, and cannot be too securely guarded by the most explicit declarations in their favor.

15. The difficulty, if not impracticability, of exercising the equal and equitable powers of government by a single legislature over an extent of territory that reaches from the Mississippi to the Western lakes, and from them to the Atlantic Ocean, is an insuperable objection to the adoption of the new system.

16. It is an undisputed fact that not one legislature in the United States had the most distant idea when they first appointed members for a convention ... that they would without any warrant from their constituents, presume on so bold and daring a stride, as ultimately to destroy the state governments, and offer a consolidated system ...

17. The first appearance of the article which declares the ratification of nine states sufficient for the establishment of the new system, wears the face of dissension, is a subversion of the union of Confederated States, and tends to the introduction of: anarchy and civil convulsions, and may be a means of involving the whole country in blood. ...

But it is needless to enumerate other instances, in which the proposed constitution appears contradictory to the first principles which ought to govern mankind; and it is equally so to enquire into the motives that induced to so bold a step as the annihilation of the independence and sovereignty of the thirteen distinct states.—They are but too obvious through the whole progress of the business, from the first shutting up the doors of the federal convention and resolving that no member should correspond with gentlemen in the different states on the subject under discussion.

And it is to be feared we shall soon see this country rushing into the extremes of confusion and violence, in consequence of the proceeding of a set of gentlemen, who disregarding the purposes of their appointment, have assumed powers unauthorized by any commission, have unnecessarily rejected the confederation of the United States, and annihilated the sovereignty and independence of the individual governments.—The causes which have inspired a few men to assemble for very different purposes with such a degree of temerity as to break with a single stroke the union of America, and disseminate the seeds of discord through the land may be easily investigated, when we survey the partizans of monarchy in the state conventions, urging the adoption of a mode of government that militates with the former professions and exertions of this country, and with all ideas of republicanism, and the equal rights of men.

CHAPTER 8

Building a Nation and an Empire

I n 1789, the newly constituted United States inaugurated its first president and convened its first session of Congress. Questions about the basic structure of national government, which had dominated public discourse since the 1770s, finally found answers in the new Constitution.

Despite this settlement, the decades that followed were anything but tranquil. The creation of federal authority forced Americans to confront questions that defined the political order of the period and the operations of the federal government for generations to come: How would the new government generate revenue and pay its debts? How far could it go to compel citizens' obedience? Could it successfully assert national sovereignty in a world of powerful, threatening empires? Within each of these debates were even bigger questions: To what extent should the United States expand its territory and authority? Would the nation remain united? Would it remain independent?

The following documents illustrate some of these major questions. In the first, George Washington bids farewell to the presidency and offers advice to his fellow citizens. Washington's remarks, which were likely drafted by Alexander Hamilton, described the dire threats many Americans felt their nation was facing.

In the second document, a prominent naturalist and congressman named Samuel Latham Mitchill considers potential names for the new nation. Although his suggestions may sound strange today, they represent an attempt to address the factional battles that concerned Washington and indicate the influence of European norms in the early United States.

In the final document, Representative Felix Grundy of Tennessee advocates for war with Great Britain. Grundy was one of many so-called War Hawks—a group of mostly southern and western congressmen who believed war was necessary to drive the British from North America, open new territory for white settlement, and ensure America's place among the world's imperial powers. Their efforts eventually led to the War of 1812.

FUNDAMENTALS

1. According to Washington, what problems faced the United States? What solutions did he propose?

2. How did Washington envision the United States' place in world affairs?

3. Why did Mitchill think it was a problem for citizens of the United States to refer to themselves as Americans?

4. Why did Grundy believe the United States needed to expand into new territory?

ANALYSIS AND INTERPRETATION

1. How did Washington understand the proper role of a citizen in a republic?

2. What did Washington mean when he referred to "liberty"? How did he understand the relationship of liberty and government?

3. Why did Mitchill want the United States to have a proper name? Why might the name's adaptability to songs and poetry have been a particular concern of his?

4. Why might Grundy and his contemporaries have described the young United States as an "empire"? How would you characterize—geopolitically, economically, militarily, etc.—Grundy's vision of empire?

5. How did Europe influence how each of these authors conceived of the young United States and the problems it faced?

George Washington, *Farewell Address* (1796)[1]

Friends and Fellow Citizens:

The period for a new election of a citizen to administer the executive government of the United States being not far distant, and the time actually arrived when your thoughts must be employed in designating the person who is to be clothed with that important trust, it appears to me proper, especially as it may conduce to a more distinct expression of the public voice, that I should now apprise you of the resolution I have formed, to decline being considered among the number of those out of whom a choice is to be made. ...

~~~

The unity of government which constitutes you one people is also now dear to you. It is justly so, for it is a main pillar in the edifice of your real independence, the support of your tranquility at home, your peace abroad; of your safety; of your prosperity; of that very liberty which you so highly prize. But as it is easy to foresee that, from different causes and from different quarters, much pains will be taken, many artifices employed to weaken in your minds the conviction of this truth; as this is the point in your political fortress against which the batteries of internal and external enemies will be most constantly and actively (though often covertly and insidiously) directed, it is of infinite moment that you should properly estimate the immense value of your national union to your collective and individual happiness; that you should cherish a cordial, habitual, and immovable attachment to it; accustoming yourselves to think and speak of it as of the palladium of your political safety and prosperity; watching for its preservation with jealous anxiety; discountenancing whatever may suggest even a suspicion that it can in any event be abandoned; and indignantly frowning upon the first dawning of every attempt to alienate any portion of our country from the rest, or to enfeeble the sacred ties which now link together the various parts.

For this you have every inducement of sympathy and interest. Citizens by birth or choice, of a common country, that country has a right to concentrate your affections. The name of American, which belongs to you in your national capacity, must always exalt the just pride of patriotism more than any appellation derived from local discriminations. With slight shades of difference, you have the same religion, manners, habits, and political principles. You have in a common cause fought and triumphed together; the independence and liberty you possess are the work of joint counsels, and joint efforts of common dangers, sufferings, and successes. ...

~~~

In contemplating the causes which may disturb our Union, it occurs as matter of serious concern that any ground should have been furnished for characterizing parties by geographical discriminations, Northern and Southern, Atlantic and Western; whence designing men may endeavor to excite a belief that there is a real difference of local interests and views. One of the expedients of party to acquire influence within particular districts is to misrepresent the opinions and aims of other districts. You cannot shield yourselves too much against the jealousies and heartburnings

---

1 From George Washington, *Farewell Address* (New York: D. Appleton and Company, 1796), 3, 6–7, 10, 11, 12–15, 20–21.

which spring from these misrepresentations; they tend to render alien to each other those who ought to be bound together by fraternal affection. ...

To the efficacy and permanency of your Union, a government for the whole is indispensable. No alliance, however strict, between the parts can be an adequate substitute; they must inevitably experience the infractions and interruptions which all alliances in all times have experienced. Sensible of this momentous truth, you have improved upon your first essay, by the adoption of a constitution of government better calculated than your former for an intimate union, and for the efficacious management of your common concerns. This government, the offspring of our own choice, uninfluenced and unawed, adopted upon full investigation and mature deliberation, completely free in its principles, in the distribution of its powers, uniting security with energy, and containing within itself a provision for its own amendment, has a just claim to your confidence and your support. Respect for its authority, compliance with its laws, acquiescence in its measures, are duties enjoined by the fundamental maxims of true liberty. The basis of our political systems is the right of the people to make and to alter their constitutions of government. But the Constitution which at any time exists, till changed by an explicit and authentic act of the whole people, is sacredly obligatory upon all. The very idea of the power and the right of the people to establish government presupposes the duty of every individual to obey the established government. ...

Towards the preservation of your government, and the permanency of your present happy state, it is requisite, not only that you steadily discountenance irregular oppositions to its acknowledged authority, but also that you resist with care the spirit of innovation upon its principles, however specious the pretexts. One method of assault may be to effect, in the forms of the Constitution, alterations which will impair the energy of the system, and thus to undermine what cannot be directly overthrown. In all the changes to which you may be invited, remember that time and habit are at least as necessary to fix the true character of governments as of other human institutions; that experience is the surest standard by which to test the real tendency of the existing constitution of a country; that facility in changes, upon the credit of mere hypothesis and opinion, exposes to perpetual change, from the endless variety of hypothesis and opinion; and remember, especially, that for the efficient management of your common interests, in a country so extensive as ours, a government of as much vigor as is consistent with the perfect security of liberty is indispensable. Liberty itself will find in such a government, with powers properly distributed and adjusted, its surest guardian. ...

I have already intimated to you the danger of parties in the State, with particular reference to the founding of them on geographical discriminations. Let me now take a more comprehensive view, and warn you in the most solemn manner against the baneful effects of the spirit of party, generally.

This spirit, unfortunately, is inseparable from our nature, having its root in the strongest passions of the human mind. It exists under different shapes in all governments, more or less stifled, controlled, or repressed; but, in those of the popular form, it is seen in its greatest rankness, and is truly their worst enemy. ...

It serves always to distract the public councils and enfeeble the public administration. It agitates the community with ill-founded jealousies and false alarms, kindles the animosity of one part against another, foments occasionally riot and insurrection. It opens the door to foreign influence and corruption, which finds a facilitated access to the government itself through the channels of party passions. Thus the policy and the will of one country are subjected to the policy and will of another.

There is an opinion, that parties in free countries are useful checks upon the administration of the government and serve to keep alive the spirit of liberty. This within certain limits is probably true; and in governments of a monarchical cast, patriotism may look with indulgence, if not with favor, upon the spirit of party. But in those of the popular character, in governments purely elective, it is a spirit not to be encouraged. From their natural tendency, it is certain there will always be enough of that spirit for every salutary purpose. And there being constant danger of excess, the effort ought to be by force of public opinion, to mitigate and assuage it. A fire not to be quenched, it demands a uniform vigilance to prevent its bursting into a flame, lest, instead of warming, it should consume. ...

~~~

Against the insidious wiles of foreign influence (I conjure you to believe me, fellow-citizens) the jealousy of a free people ought to be constantly awake, since history and experience prove that foreign influence is one of the most baneful foes of republican government. But that jealousy to be useful must be impartial; else it becomes the instrument of the very influence to be avoided, instead of a defense against it. Excessive partiality for one foreign nation and excessive dislike of another cause those whom they actuate to see danger only on one side, and serve to veil and even second the arts of influence on the other. Real patriots who may resist the intrigues of the favorite are liable to become suspected and odious, while its tools and dupes usurp the applause and confidence of the people, to surrender their interests.

The great rule of conduct for us in regard to foreign nations is in extending our commercial relations, to have with them as little political connection as possible. So far as we have already formed engagements, let them be fulfilled with perfect good faith. Here let us stop. Europe has a set of primary interests which to us have none; or a very remote relation. Hence she must be engaged in frequent controversies, the causes of which are essentially foreign to our concerns. Hence, therefore, it must be unwise in us to implicate ourselves by artificial ties in the ordinary vicissitudes of her politics, or the ordinary combinations and collisions of her friendships or enmities.

Our detached and distant situation invites and enables us to pursue a different course. If we remain one people under an efficient government, the period is not far off when we may defy material injury from external annoyance; when we may take such an attitude as will cause the neutrality we may at any time resolve upon to be scrupulously respected; when belligerent nations, under the impossibility of making acquisitions upon us, will not lightly hazard the giving us provocation; when we may choose peace or war, as our interest, guided by justice, shall counsel.

Why forego the advantages of so peculiar a situation? Why quit our own to stand upon foreign ground? Why, by interweaving our destiny with that of any part of Europe, entangle our peace and prosperity in the toils of European ambition, rivalship, interest, humor or caprice?

United States, 19th September, 1796

Geo. Washington

Samuel Latham Mitchill, "Generic Names for the Country and People of the United States of America" (1803)[2]

The portion of terraqueous globe comprehended by the great Lakes, the Saint Lawrence, the Ocean and the Mississippi, has no general denomination by which it can be conveniently distinguished in geography. Its subdivisions and local names are appropriate enough and sufficiently well understood. But there is still wanting one broad and universal appellation, to designate and characterize the whole appropriated and unappropriated territory of the United States.

It was a great oversight in the Convention of 1787, that they did not give a name to the country for which they devised a frame of government. Its citizens are suffering every day for lack of such a generic term. Destitute of a proper name for their own soil and region, they express themselves vaguely and awkwardly on the subject. By some it is termed "United States"; this however is a *political*, and not a *geographical* title. By others it is called "America," and the inhabitants "Americans." But these epithets equally belong to Labrador and Paraguay and their natives. "New-England" and "New-Englanders" are two uncouth terms applied by certain other writers and speakers. In some parts of Europe, we have been distinguished as "Anglo-Americans"; and this appellation is in some respects worse, and in no respect better than either of the others.

What are we to do? Are we never to have a geographical distinction? Is the land to be forever called "United States," and its people "United-Statesmen?" And even then, on a supposition that the union should cease must the region it occupies be nameless?

It is in the power of the people to find and adopt fitting names for their country and themselves, by common consent. These ought to be expressive, concise, nervous and poetical. And any new word possessing these qualities, may serve to designate *this part of the planet we inhabit.*— From such a word as a radical term, all others proper for distinguishing the people, &c. may be derived.

To supply this sad deficiency in our geographical and national nomenclature, the following project is respectfully submitted to the consideration of our map-makers, engravers, printers, legislators and men of letters. The authors of it are citizens of the United States, and are zealous for their prosperity, honour, and reputation. They wish them to possess a name among the nations of the earth. They lament that hitherto and at present the country is destitute of one.

Let the extent of land ceded to our nation by the treaty of 1783, be distinguished henceforward on charts, globes, and in elementary books by the name of

2   From "Generic Names for the Country and People of the United States of America," *The Monthly Anthology, and Boston Review* 1 (June 1804), 342–345.

FREDON:

the etymology of this is obvious and agreeable: it may mean a *free-gift;* or any *thing done freely;* or *the land of free privileges and doings.* This is the proper term to be employed in all grave, solemn, and prose compositions, and in ordinary conversation. It is better adapted than "Albion" is to England

If, however, any of the favorites of the Muses desire a poetical name for this tract of earth, it is easy to supply them with one which sounds and pronounces to great advantage. Such an one is

FREDONIA:

which will meet the ear more excellently than Italia, Gallia, Parthia, Hispania, Germania, or even Britannia itself.—America and Columbia will retain their present signification of extending to the whole Western hemisphere.

The citizens and inhabitants of the United States when spoken of generally, without reference to any particular state, may be known and distinguished as

FREDONIANS.

And that such a person being asked in Europe or any other part of the world, from what country he comes or to what nation he belongs, may correctly and precisely answer that he is a FREDONIAN. And this will meet the ear much more nobly than "a Frenchman, a Spaniard, a Portuguese," "a Turk" and the like.

Again, a monosyllable name is perfectly easy to be obtained from the same root; and to him who thinks the last word too long or lofty, it will be wholly at his option to call himself

FREDE;

and in this respect he will put himself on a par with a "Mede" and "a Swede."

Moreover, should an adjective be desired to qualify expressions and facilitate discourse, there is such a thing immediately ready for use in

FREDISH;

and thereby, we can speak of "a Fredish ship," or a "Fredishman," or a "Fredish manufacture or production," after the same manner and according to the same rule, by which we employ the adjectives, *British, Spanish, Danish, Turkish,* and the like.

Thus, our nation is in possession of a *prosaic* word for its whole territory, FREDON; a *poetical* word for the same, FREDONIA; a *grave and sonorous* generic title for its people, property and relations, FREDONIAN; a *short and colloquial appellation*, FREDE; and a convenient universal epithet, FREDISH. A language so rich and copious is scarcely to be found; and it is hoped our citizens will make the most of it.

In case any of our countrymen should wish to express himself according to this novel dialect, the following is offered as an example, alluding to a recent subject of public discussion.

"It has been a favourite object with a certain class of men to involve FREDON in a war with Spain, France or both of them, about the right of deposit on the Mississippi. The outrageous conduct of the Intendant at New-Orleans was indeed very provoking, but the FREDONIAN SPIRIT, though roused by just indignation, was too temperate and magnanimous to rush immediately to arms. It was thought most wise and politic for the administration to attempt a negociation in the first instance, and accordingly, one of the FREDISH ships was ordered to be got in readiness to carry an envoy extraordinary from America to Europe. Should war become necessary for the national honour and security, our public enemies will find to their sorrow that the FREDES will make brave soldiers and gallant sailors. Never will they quit the hardy contest until their deeds shall be worthy of being recorded in immortal verse, equally honourable to the bards and the heroes of FREDONIA."

The radical word is also well adapted to songs and rhymes. And this is a great convenience and felicity in a national point of view. Observe, how prettily our poets can make it jingle: for instance, if the subject is warlike, then

> "Their Chiefs, to glory lead on
> "The noble sons of FREDON."

Or if it is moral sublimity,

> "Nor Plato, in his PHAEDON
> Excels the Sage of FREDON."

Should it be commercial activity,

> "All Nations have agreed on
> The enterprise of FREDON."

Perhaps it may refer to our exports; why then

> "The Portuguese may feed on
> The wheat and maize of FREDON."

It may be desirable to celebrate our agriculture, as in the following distich,

> "No land so good as FREDON
> To scatter grain and seed on."

On the supposition that a swain wishes to compliment his country-women, he may inform them that

> "The graceful nymphs of FREDON
> Surpass all belles we read on."

And indeed if it is desire to ejaculate in a serious strain, it may be written,

> "In this fair land of FREDON
> May right and justice be done."

We give these as samples of what may be accomplished in this way, adding that the poet may easily contrast his country with SWEDEN, or compare it to EDEN, if he is puzzled for a rhyme.

On the whole, we recommend these words to the serious consideration and speedy adoption of our fellow-citizens; that our common and beloved portion of the earth, may thereby acquire a NAME, and be famous among the NATIONS.

Speech of Representative Felix Grundy
(of Tennessee) in Congress (1811)[3]

What, Mr. Speaker, are we now called on to decide? It is, whether we will resist by force the attempt, made by the Government, to subject our maritime rights to the arbitrary and capricious rule of her will; for my part I am not prepared to say that this country shall submit to have her commerce interdicted or regulated, by any foreign nation. Sir, I prefer war to submission.

Over and above these unjust pretensions of the British Government, for many years past they have been in the practice of impressing our seamen, from merchant vessels; this unjust and lawless invasion of personal liberty, calls loudly for the interposition of this Government. To those better acquainted with the facts in relation to it, I leave it to fill up the picture. My mind is irresistibly drawn to the West.

Although others may not strongly feel the bearing which the late transactions in that quarter have on this subject, upon my mind they have great influence. It cannot be believed by any man who will reflect, that the savage tribes, uninfluenced by other Powers, would think of making war on the United States. They understand too well their own weakness, and our strength. They have already felt the weight of our arms; they know they hold the very soil on which they live as tenants at sufferance. How, then, sir, are we to account for their late conduct? In one way only; some powerful nation must have intrigued with them, and turned their peaceful disposition towards us into hostilities. Great Britain alone has intercourse with those Northern tribes; I therefore infer, that if British gold has not been employed, their baubles and trinkets, and the promise of support and a place of refuge if necessary, have had their effect.

If I am right in this conjecture, war is not to commence by sea of land, it is already begun; and some of the richest blood of our country has already been shed. Yes, Mr. Speaker, in one individual has fallen, the honest man, the orator, and the soldier. That he loved his country none can doubt—he died to preserve its honor and its fame—I mean the late commander of the cavalry; you sir, who have often measured your strength with his in forensic debate, can attest that he in a good degree, was the pride of the Western country, and Kentucky claimed him as a favorite son. For his loss, with those who fell by his side, the whole Western country is ready to march; they only wait for our permission; and sir, war once declared, I pledge myself for my people—they will avenge the death of their brethren.

Another consideration drawn from our past conduct demands the course we have proposed. In the year 1808, Congress declared that this nation had but three alternatives left—war, embargo, or submission; since that time no advantageous change has taken place in our foreign relations; we now have no embargo, we have not declared war. I then say it, with humiliation, produced by the degradation of my country, we have submitted. Mr. Speaker, I derive no pleasure from speaking in this way of my country, but it is true, and, however painful the truth may be, it should be told.

---

3   From *Annals of Congress, 12th Congress, 1st Session* (Washington: Library of Congress, December 1811), 422–427.

Another reason operates in my mind; we stand pledged to the French nation to continue in force our non-importation law against Britain; without a violation of national faith we cannot repeal it. What effects is the operation of this law producing? It is demoralizing our citizens; men of commercial habits cannot easily change their course of life; those who have lived in affluence and ease cannot consent to beg for bread. No, sir, they will violate this law, they will smuggle; and, sir, in politics, as in private life, if you wish men to remain virtuous, lead them not into temptation.

This restrictive system operates unequally; some parts of the Union enjoy the same advantages which they possessed when no difficulties attended our foreign relations; others suffer extremely. Ask the Northern man, and he will tell you that any state of things is better than the present; inquire of the Western people why their crops are not equal to what they were in former years, they will answer that industry has no stimulus left, since their surplus products have no markets. Notwithstanding these objections to the present restrictive system, we are bound to retain it—this, and our plighted faith to the French Government, have tied the Gordian knot; we cannot untie it; we can cut it with the sword.

This war, if carried on successfully, will have its advantages. We shall drive the British from our Continent—they will no longer have an opportunity of intriguing our Indian neighbors, and setting on the ruthless savage to tomahawk our women and children. That nation will lose her Canadian trade, and, by having no resting place in this country, her means of annoying us will be diminished. The idea I am now about to advance is at war, I know, with sentiments of the gentleman from Virginia: I am willing to receive the Canadians as adopted brethren; it will have beneficial political effects; it will preserve the equilibrium of the Government. When Louisiana shall be fully people, the Northern States will lose their power; they will be at the discretion of others; they can be depressed at pleasure, and then this Union might be endangered—I therefore feel anxious not only to add the Floridas to the South, but the Canadas to the North of this empire.

PART III

A House Dividing

CHAPTER 9

Liberty and Democracy in the Age of Market Revolution

The early nineteenth century was a time of dynamic change in the United States. Military victories over Native Americans and sustained diplomatic efforts continued to open the American West for white settlement. Improvements in transportation and communication bound the nation together and drove the rapid advance of commercial society. For increasing numbers of Americans, the rhythms and demands of market capitalism came to structure their everyday lives like never before.

For some Americans, these changes brought fear and anxiety. Protestant clergymen following Lyman Beecher objected that America's rising affluence had not been accompanied by an increase in piety and morality. Especially for a nation in which ordinary citizens chose political leaders, grave dangers abounded. Only through the widespread revival of Christian religiosity would America's democracy be saved from destruction.

Uncertainties aside, many Americans celebrated this era as one of great opportunity. Born in Ireland to a middling family, Mathew Carey migrated to Philadelphia in 1784. With the financial backing of others, he established a publishing business and soon achieved financial success and national notoriety. Carey retired in the early 1820s and turned much of his attention to philanthropic endeavors, which included counseling the less fortunate about how to achieve economic success in the young American republic.

Not all Americans, however, shared equally in the age's riches. For many artisans and urban workers, market society spurred concentrations of wealth that threatened their ability to become independent, property-owning citizens. Many sought opportunities elsewhere, but others remained in America's growing cities and called for reform. Chief among their demands was the expansion of voting rights for the expanding population of propertyless white males. Throughout the period, state constitutional conventions became theaters of democracy where Americans reassessed key parameters of the political order.

The age of market revolution also transformed women's lives, perhaps nowhere more acutely than in the textile factories that sprung up in New England. The thousands of young women who flocked to the mills became some of America's first industrial workers. In the process, they gained a degree of independence as they earned wages and lived apart from traditional communal and familial oversight. Amid the era's vast transformations, some women began to demand that they too be afforded the right to vote in America's democracy.

FUNDAMENTALS

1. According to Lyman Beecher, what threats imperiled American democracy in 1831?

2. Which of Mathew Carey's suggestions did you find most surprising? Why?

3. According to the Virginia petitioners, how did "freeholders" justify their suffrage while restricting nonfreeholders' right to vote?

4. According to Baker, what were the challenges of factory life?

5. What arguments did the Jefferson County petitioners make in favor of women's suffrage?

ANALYSIS AND INTERPRETATION

1. How might the socioeconomic transformations that occurred during this era have shaped the calls for increased religiosity and political rights?

2. Why did Lyman Beecher think religious revivals were so vitally important to the survival of American democracy?

3. How did Mathew Carey seem to understand the sources of success and wealth in American society? How would you characterize his advice for impoverished Americans?

4. How might the Virginia memorialists have responded to Mathew Carey's recommendations?

5. How would you characterize Josephine Baker's description of the mills and her assessment of their effect on women's lives?

6. To what extent did the women of Jefferson County echo the Virginia memorialists?

Lyman Beecher, "The Necessity of Revivals of Religion to the Perpetuity of Our Civil and Religious Institutions" (1831)[1]

The dangers which threaten these United States, and the free institutions here established, are numerous and appalling. They arise, in part, from our vast extent of territory, our numerous and increasing population, from diversity of local interests, the power of selfishness, and the fury of sectional jealousy and hate. All these are powerful causes of strife, and never were they in more powerful or terrific action.

These causes, alone sufficient to set on fire the course of nature, have, during several of the last years, been wielded, concentrated, and blown into fury, by a mad ambition. The thirst of power and dominion has fallen upon some of our leading politicians, to whom the ordinary elements of strife seem tame and lazy in the work of ruin; and they—regardless of consequences, and with a view to subserve their own political ends—have heated the furnace of anger seven-fold, and raised to a seven-fold height the winds and waves of political commotion.

To these must be added the corrupting influences of a pre-eminent national prosperity, productive of voluptuousness, extravagance, and rash speculation, and leading, in many instances, to reckless poverty and misery.

The increase of intellectual power too, without a corresponding increase of moral restraint, and this connected with the universality of suffrage, presents an ocean of unstable mind to the ruthless power of mad ambition. ...

Another danger not to be overlooked, arises from the intrigues of Catholic Europe, through the medium of our own Catholic population, to give a predominance to their religion with all its anti-republican tendencies, and thus to divide us, and destroy our institutions.

Such are some of the dangers which threaten us. And they are not fictitious; nor are they trifles magnified for rhetorical effect. The language I have employed is indeed strong language, but it falls unmeasurably below the amplitude and imminence of the evils which have been described. ... Unless some subduing, tranquilizing influence can be applied, superior to all which man can apply, our race as a nation is swift, and our destruction sure.

Let me then call the attention of my readers to *our only remaining source of hope*—God—*and the interpositions of his Holy Spirit, in great and general Revivals of Religion, to reform the hearts of this people, and make the nation good and happy.*

There is for us assuredly but one remedy, and that is, such a state of the affections towards God and our neighbor, as the Law and the Gospel require:—Not the ascendancy of Christians over the world, but the world, in the day of God's power, becoming Christian. The influence which is necessary to save us is the influence of truth, made effectual by the supernatural influence

---

1   From "The Necessity of Revivals of Religion to the Perpetuity of Our Civil and Religious Institutions," *Spirit of the Pilgrims* 4 (September 1831), 467–479.

of God's Holy Spirit ... It is not to be supposed a thing beyond the power of God, to effect such a change of human character as will reconcile universal liberty and boundless prosperity, with their permanence and purity. ...

The government of God is the only government which will hold society, against depravity within and temptation without; and this it must do by the force of its own law written upon the heart. This is that unity of the Spirit and the bond of peace which alone can perpetuate national purity and tranquility—that law of universal and impartial love by which alone nations can be kept back from ruin. There is no safety for republics but in self-government, under the influence of a holy heart, swayed by the government of God.

But even these principles of national conservation, to avail, must become immensely more extensive and operative than they have been or are; for it is not the church which is to govern the world, but the world must become Christian and govern itself. ...The renovating power must then operate on greater masses of mind ... A few drops in the Mississippi might as well attempt to stop and turn back the whole descending flood, as Christianity attempt, in its present state, to turn the public sentiment of the nation. The wicked will do wickedly, and will claim the right to do so, without the hindrance of law or shame, and there is no stopping the insurrection, but as the hearts of men, by the grace of God, shall be radically changed.

Since the overthrow of Puritan public sentiment, it is only recently that Christian principles have been thought of, as exerting any influence in national policy. And the first indication of such intrusion of conscience and principle, has been met with sneers and contumely in the halls of national legislation, while it has sent alarm through the ranks of worldliness and sin. An eternity of such slow-paced and limited success, as has for centuries past attended the preaching of the Gospel, would leave the nation still under the dominion of the powers of darkness.

We have fallen upon other times than the church of God ever saw before ... Old foundations are broken up, and old principles and maxims are undergoing a thorough and perilous revision, and that too upon a mighty scale.

In our colonial state we were few, and poor, and feeble. Intercourse was difficult and rare, and moral causes insulated and local. What was said in one colony was not heard in another, and what was done in one state was not felt in another. But now, each colony is a state, and each state a nation, and intercourse is rapid, and local causes tell in their results throughout the whole, as every stroke on the body is felt through all its members. Nations compose our confederacy, and nations our religious denominations, and nations the army of the aliens. Since then such new and increased action has commenced, for the moral energies of religion to be stationary, is relatively to retrograde to imbecility and insignificance. The relative increase of unconverted population, by birth and emigration and irreligious and corrupting influence, without a corresponding increase of divine influence to render the government of God effectual, would supersede the persecution of the church only by placing her in such obscurity, as to be overlooked both by fear and by hate.

Some who ... think it most desirable that conversions should be rather dilatory and gradual, than sudden and multitudinous, forget that the revivals in the kingdom of darkness are moving on with terrific haste and power. Millions are bursting into that kingdom, while hundreds only are added to the kingdom of Christ. It is not time for ministers to think themselves faithful and successful without revivals. ... On steamboats, and canals, and railroads, and turnpikes, the ungodly are gathering together against the sacramental host, to obliterate the Sabbath, and raze Zion to her foundations. Nothing but the power of Almighty God can sustain the churches in this tremendous conflict. Nothing but speedy, extensive, and powerful revivals of religion can save our nation from impending ruin. ... Nothing but a phalanx of holy hearts around the Sabbath can save it. Nothing but such a national change of heart and affections as will cause the Sabbath to become a delight, and the sanctuary of the Lord honorable, can preserve our institutions from desecration and ruin. In the day of God's power, the nation must become willing to obey him, or its destruction is inevitable.

The revival of real holiness never commences and moves on in a congregation, or town, or city, without a strong reacting sensation;—and it is only by the prostrating rapidity of revivals, that the infuriated resistance of persecution can be superseded. ... Religion, real heartfelt religion, is to become, at no distant day, the predominant characteristic of man, the governing principle of empires and of the world. ...

The political renovation of the world by revolutions will demand enterprise, and treasure, and blood. But the whole boundless sacrifice and victory will be a wanton waste of life and treasure, unless Christianity, with its healing and tranquilizing power, may follow the shock of battles, and staunch the flowing blood, and bind up the wounds of a bleeding world. But to do this, no accidental effort will suffice ... The world itself must be aroused,—the Redeemed and emancipated part, to enlighten and emancipate those that sit in darkness and the region of the shadow of death. The emancipation of man—the intellectual, political and moral emancipation of the world, must engross the desires, and concentrate the wisdom, the charity, and the enterprise of the world itself. ...

For more than thirty years, there have been a series of revivals in our land, with increasing power, extent and frequency ... Generally, they have been free from enthusiasm and excess—have been seasons of silent attention and deep feeling, of clear, intellectual, argumentative, doctrinal preaching, with pungent applications to the conscience, attended with deep convictions of sin, and with subsequent joy and peace in believing. Their effects upon religion and morals have been most auspicious. They have furnished, probably, three fourths of the living ministry of the evangelical churches of our land, and nearly three fourths of the members of these churches. They have reared and sustained the family altar, and trained up the rising generation in the nurture and admonition of the Lord. They have provided hearts, and hands, and means, to superintend the manifold ministrations required to organize infant and Sabbath schools, and all our benevolent voluntary associations. Thirty years ago, it was a rare thing to meet with a young person in the church; and now, more than half the professors of religion are in early life. And it may be truly said, that almost the entire moral energy by which the cause of Christ now moves on from conquering to conquer, is the result of those revivals of religion which for thirty years have been enrolling, augmenting and disciplining the sacramental host. ...

... We doubt not that greater revivals than have been are indispensable, to save our nation, and to save the world, by giving universal and saving empire to the kingdom of Christ; and as clouds thicken and dangers press, we look for them with strong confidence, and with the increased urgency of unutterable desire.

Mathew Carey, *Advices and Suggestions to Increase the Comforts of Persons in Humble Circumstance* (1832)[2]

1. Avoid all unnecessary expenses, however small.

2. There is no nourishment in tea, and but little in coffee.

3. A comfortable, nourishing meal of mush and molasses would not cost as much for four persons, as a breakfast of tea or coffee for three, perhaps for two.

4. Rice is far more nutritious than wheat flour. Rice and molasses make a very cheap and nutritious food.

5. There is but little nourishment in gingerbread, in proportion to the cost. Do not pamper your children with it: it injures the stomach. Three cents a day for gingerbread are above ten dollars a year; two a day, above seven dollars. Many poor families give that quantity to each child. If you must give them cakes, let them have crackers. There is at least twice the nourishment in them, in proportion to the cost.

6. Segars, spirits, and tobacco, in many poor families, cost more than clothes for their children. Three glasses of spirits, at three cents each, and six segars, at three for a cent, come to above forty dollars a year. How many families, bowed down by pinching poverty, purchase more of each of them! How much distress would the sum remove, and how much comfort it would afford! Dram-drinking is the sure "road to ruin." Renounce it, as you value your happiness here and hereafter. Shame, and disgrace, and infamy, and disease are its attendants. ... Three-fourths of those who are addicted to the vile vice, are miserable and wretched; and, after entailing misery and wretchedness on their families, generally close their career in alms-houses. Let this frightful result be constantly in your mind, as an admonition to sobriety.

7. Make an effort to purchase your necessaries for cash. This will produce two good effects— You will purchase nothing but what you actually want, and what you do purchase, you will procure on better terms. ...

8. Should you have a few dollars, or even a single dollar, to spare, avail yourself of the Saving Fund immediately. There your money will be safe, and not only safe, but bring you interest; whereas, if retained, it might, and probably would, as the children say, "burn a hole in your pocket."...

10. In the purchase of clothing for yourself or your family, avoid spending any thing on fashion. Get good, cheap, strong, lasting stuff, and have it made up plainly.

11. Have your room or rooms whitewashed twice a year. It not only inspires habits of decency, but conduces to health, and prevents the growth of vermin.

12. Stewed meat is far more nutritious than boiled or roasted. The roasting, or boiling, (unless, in the latter case, soup is made) extracts and loses a considerable portion of the nourishing juices of the meat. Soup is a most economical food, and should be used twice or thrice a week.

---

2   From Mathew Carey, *Advices and Suggestions to Increase the Comforts of Persons in Humble Circumstance* (Philadelphia: Mathew Carey, 1832).

13. Whenever you are sick, apply to some of your neighbours for a recommendation to the Dispensary of your district. Doctors' bills are ruinous to the poor.[3]

14. Never be idle. Employ every leisure hour, or half or quarter of an hour, in reading good books, moral, religious, or historical, if you can procure them, or in instructing your children.

15. Send your children to the infant or public schools as early as their age will permit. Let them always go washed and combed, and with their clothes mended, if necessary.

16. Avoid all species of gambling, whether in lottery tickets, or otherwise. The hopes of gain held out are delusive.

---

3 Established by civic leaders, philanthropists, and doctors, dispensaries were the dominant way that poor urbanites accessed medical care throughout the nineteenth century.

The Memorial of the Non-Freeholders of the City of Richmond, Respectfully Addressed to the Convention, Now Assembled to Deliberate on Amendments of the State Constitution (1830)[4]

Your memorialists ... belong to that class of citizens, who, not having the good fortune to possess a certain portion of land, are, for that cause only, debarred from the enjoyment of the right of suffrage. Experience has but too clearly evinced, what, indeed, reason had always foretold, by how frail a tenure they hold every other right, who are denied this, the highest prerogative of freemen. The want of it has afforded both the pretext and the means of excluding the entire class, to which your memorialists belong, from all participation in the recent election of the body, they now respectfully address. Comprising a very large part, probably a majority of male citizens of mature age, they have been passed by, like aliens or slaves, as if destitute of interest, or unworthy of a voice, in measures involving their future political destiny: whilst the freeholders, sole possessors, under the existing Constitution, of the elective franchise, have, upon the strength of that possession alone, asserted and maintained in themselves, the exclusive power of new-modelling the fundamental laws of the State: in other words, have seized upon the sovereign authority.

It cannot be necessary, in addressing the Convention now assembled, to expatiate on the momentous importance of the right of suffrage, or to enumerate the evils consequent upon its unjust limitation. ... Among the doctrines inculcated in the great charter handed down to us, as a declaration of the rights pertaining to the good people of Virginia and their posterity, "as the basis and foundation of Government," we are taught,

"That all men are by nature equally free and independent, and have certain inherent rights, of which, when they enter into a state of society, they cannot, by any compact, deprive or divest their posterity: namely, the enjoyment of life and liberty, with the means of acquiring and possessing property, and pursuing and obtaining happiness and safety.

"That all power is vested in, and consequently derived from, the people.

"That a majority of the community hath an indisputable, unalienable, and indefeasible right to reform, alter or abolish the Government.

"That no man, nor set of men, are entitled to exclusive or separate emoluments or privileges, but in consideration of public services.

"That all men, having sufficient evidence of permanent common interest with, and attachment to, the community, have a right of suffrage, and cannot be taxed, or deprived of their property, without their consent, or that of their representative, nor bound by any law, to which they have not, in like manner, assented, for the public good."

---

4   From *Proceedings and Debates of the Virginia State Convention of 1829–1830* (Richmond: Samuel Shepherd & Co., 1830), 25–31.

How do the principles thus proclaimed, accord with the existing regulation of suffrage? A regulation, which, instead of the equality nature ordains, creates an odious distinction between members of the same community; robs of all share in the enactment of the laws, a large portion of the citizens, bound by them, and whose blood and treasure are pledged to maintain them, and vests in a favored class, not in consideration of their public services, but of their private possessions, the highest of all privileges: one which, as is now in flagrant proof, if it does not constitute, at least is held, practically to confer, absolute sovereignty. ...

... To ascribe to a landed possession, moral or intellectual endowments, would truly be regarded as ludicrous, were it not for the gravity with which the proposition is maintained, and still more for the grave consequences flowing from it. Such possession no more proves him who has it, wiser or better, than it proves him taller or stronger, than him who has it not. That cannot be a fit criterion for the exercise of any right, the possession of which does not indicate the existence, nor the want of it the absence, of any essential qualification. ...

Virtue, intelligence, are not among the products of the soil. Attachment to property, often a sordid sentiment, is not to be confounded with the sacred flame of patriotism. The love of country, like that of parents and offspring, is engrafted in our nature. It exists in all climates, among all classes, under every possible form of Government. Riches oftener impair it than poverty. Who has it not is a monster.

To be deprived of their rightful equality, and to hear as an apology that they are too ignorant and vicious to enjoy it, is no ordinary trial of patience. Yet they will suppress the indignant emotions these sweeping denunciations are well calculated to excite. The freeholders themselves know them to be unfounded: Why, else, are arms placed in the hands of a body of disaffected citizens, so ignorant, so depraved, and so numerous? In the hour of danger, they have drawn no invidious distinctions between the sons of Virginia. The muster rolls have undergone no scrutiny, no comparison with the land books, with a view to expunge those who have been struck form the ranks of freemen. If the landless citizens have been ignominiously driven from the polls, in time of peace, they have at least been generously summoned, in war, to the battle-field. ...

But, it is said, yield them this right, and they will abuse it: property, that is, landed property, will be rendered insecure, or at least overburthened, by those who possess it not. The freeholders, on the contrary, can pass no law to the injury of any other class, which will not more injuriously affect themselves. The alarm is sounded too, of danger from large manufacturing institutions, that one corrupt individual may sway the corrupt votes of thousands. ... The danger of abuse is a dangerous plea. ... If we are sincerely republican, we must give our confidence to the principles we profess. We have been taught by our fathers, that all power is vested in, and derived from , the people; not the freeholders: that the majority of the community, in whom abides the physical force, have also the political right of creating and remolding at will, their civil institutions. Nor can this right be anywhere more safely deposited. ...

The example of almost every other State in the Union, in which the patrician pretensions of the landholder have, since their foundation, been unknown or despised, in many of which, too, manufacturing institutions exist on an extensive scale, ought alone to dispel these visionary fears of danger from the people. Indeed, all history demonstrates that the many have oftener been the victims than the oppressors. Cunning has proved an over-match for strength. The few have but too well succeeded in convincing them of their incapacity to manage their own affairs; and having persuaded them, for their own good, to submit to the curb, have generously taken the reins, and naturally enough converted them into beasts of burden.

But if justice is not to be expected, if self-aggrandizement is to be assumed as the sole ruling principle of men in power, then, your memorialists conceive the interests of the many deserve at least as much to be guarded as those of the few. Conceding the truth of the proposition assumed, what security, they would enquire, is there against the injustice of the freeholders? ...

Still it is said, the non-freeholders have no just cause of complaint. A freehold is easily acquired. The right of suffrage, moreover, is not a natural right. Society may grant, modify, or withhold it, as expediency may require. Indeed all agree that certain regulations are proper: those, for example, relating to age, sex, and citizenship. At best, it is an idle contest for an abstract right whose loss is attended with no practical evil. ...

... But say it is not a natural right. Whence did the freeholders derive it? How become its exclusive possessors? Will they arrogantly tell us they own the country, because they hold the land? ... Will they rely on the Constitutional provision? That was the act of men delegated by themselves. They exercised the very right in question in appointing the body from whom they profess to derive it, and indeed gave to that body all the power it possessed. What is this but to say they generously conferred the privilege upon themselves?

Let us concede that the right of suffrage is a social right; that it must of necessity be regulated by society. Still the question recurs, is the existing limitation proper? For obvious reasons, by almost universal consent, women and children, aliens and slaves, are excluded. It were useless to discuss the propriety of a rule that scarcely admits of diversity of opinion. What is concurred in by those who constitute the society, the body politic, must be taken to be right. But the exclusion of these classes for reasons peculiarly applicable to them, is no argument for excluding others to whom no one of those reasons applies.

Never can your memorialists agree that pecuniary burdens or personal violence are the sole injuries of which men may dare to complain. It may be that the freeholders have shown no disposition greatly to abuse the power they have assumed. They may have borne themselves with exemplary moderation. But their unrepresented brethren cannot submit to a degrading regulation which takes from them, on the supposition of mental inferiority or moral depravity, all share in the Government under which they live. They cannot yield to pretensions of political superiority founded on the possession of a bit of land of whatever dimensions. They cannot acquiesce in political bondage, because those who affect to sway over them the rod of empire, treat them leniently. The privilege which they claim, they respectfully insist, is theirs as of right; and they are under no obligation to assign any reason whatever for claiming it, but that is their own. ...

In behalf of the meeting,   Walter D. Blair, *Chairman*

Josephine L. Baker, "A Second Peep at Factory Life" (1845)[5]

There is an old saying, that "When we are with the Romans, we must do as the Romans do." And now, kind friend, as we are about to renew our walk, I beg that you will give heed to it, and do as factory girls do. ...

There is the "counting-room," a long, low, brick building, and opposite is the "store-house"... Between them, swings the ponderous gate that shuts the mills in from the world without. But, stop; we must get "a pass," ere we go through, or "the watchman will be after us." Having obtained this, we will stop on the slight elevation by the gate, and view the mills. The one to the left rears high its huge sides of brick and mortar, and the belfry, towering far above the rest, stands out in bold relief against the rosy sky. The almost innumerable windows glitter, like gems, in the morning sunlight. It is six and a half stories high, and, like the fabled monster of old, who guarded the sacred waters of Mars, it seems to guard its less aspiring sister to the right; that is five and a half stories high ...

We will just look into the first room. It is used for cleaning cloth. You see the scrubbing and scouring machines are in full operation, and gigging and fulling are going on in full perfection. ... In the second room the cloth is "*finished*," going through the various operations of burling, shearing, brushing, inking, fine-drawing, pressing, and packing for market. This is the pleasantest room on the corporation, and consequently they are never in want of help. The shearing, brushing, pressing and packing is done by males, while the burling, inking, marking and fine-drawing is performed by females. We will pass to the third room, called the "cassimere weaving-room," where all kinds of cloths are woven, from plain to the most exquisite fancy. There are between eighty and ninety looms, and part of the dressing is also done here. The fourth is the "broad weaving-room," and contains between thirty and forty looms; and broad sure enough they are. ... Now if you please we will go up to the next room, where the spinning is done. Here we have spinning jacks or jennies that dance merrily along whizzing and singing, as they spin out their "long yarns," and it seems but pleasure to watch their movements; but it is hard work, and requires good health and much strength. ... You appear surprised at the hurry and bustle now going on in the room, but your attention has been so engaged that you have forgotten the hour. Just look at the clock, and you will find that it wants but five minutes to "bell time."

There is a group of girls yonder, going our way; let us overtake them, and hear what they are talking about. Something unpleasant I dare say, from their earnest gestures and clouded brows.

"Well, I do think it is too bad," exclaims one.

"So do I," says another. "This cutting down wages *is not* what they cry it up to be. I wonder how they'd like to work as hard as we do, digging and drudging day after day, from morning till night, and then, every two or three years, have their wages reduced. I rather guess it wouldn't set very well."

---

5 From J. L. B., "A Second Peep at Factory Life," *Lowell* (MA) *Offering* 5 (May 1845), 97–100.

"And, besides this, who ever heard, of such a thing as their being raised again," says the first speaker. "I confess that I never did, so long as I've worked in the mill, and that's been these ten years."

"Well, it is real provoking any how," returned the other, "for my part I should think they had made a clean sweep this time. I wonder what they'll do next."

You ask, if there are so many things objectionable, why we work in the mill. Well, simply for this reason,—every situation in life, has its trials which must be borne, and factory life has no more than any other. There are many things we do not like; many occurrences that send the warm blood mantling to the cheek when they must be borne in silence, and many harsh words and acts that are not called for. There are objections also to the number of hours we work, to the length of time allotted to our meals, and to the low wages allowed for labor; objections that must and will be answered; for the time has come when something, besides the clothing and feeding of the body is to be thought of; when the mind is to be clothed and fed; and this cannot be as it should be, with the present system of labor. Who, let me ask, can find that pleasure in life which they should, when it is spent in this way. Without time for the laborer's own work, and the improvement of the mind, save the few evening hours; and even then if the mind is enriched and stored with useful knowledge, it must be at the expense of health. And the feeling too, that comes over us (there is no use in denying it) when we hear the bell calling us away from repose that tired nature loudly claims—the feeling, that we are *obliged to go.* And these few hours, of which we have spoken, are far too short, three at the most at the close of day. Surely, methinks, every heart that lays claim to humanity will feel 'tis not enough. But this, we hope will, ere long, be done away with, and labor made what it should be; pleasant and inviting to every son and daughter of the human family.

There is a brighter side to this picture, over which we would not willingly pass without notice, and an answer to the question, why we work here? The time we *do* have is our own. The money we earn comes promptly; more so than in any other situation; and our work, though laborious is the same from day to day; we know what it is, and when finished we feel perfectly free, till it is time to commence it again.

Besides this, there are many pleasant associations connected with factory life, that are not to be found elsewhere.

There are lectures, evening schools and libraries, to which all may have access. The one thing needful here, is the time to improve them as we ought.

There is a class, of whom I would speak, that work in the mills, and will while they continue in operation. Namely, the many who have no home, and who come here to seek, in this busy, bustling "City of Spindles," a competency that shall enable them in after life, to live without being a burden to society,—the many who toil on, without a murmur, for the support of an aged mother or orphaned brother and sister. For the sake of them, we earnestly hope labor may be reformed; that the miserable, selfish spirit of competition, now in our midst, may be thrust from us and consigned to eternal oblivion.

There is one other thing that must be mentioned ere we part, that is the practice of sending agents through the country to decoy girls away from their homes with the promise of high wages, when the market is already stocked to overflowing. This is certainly wrong, for it lessens the value of labor, which should be ever held in high estimation, as the path marked out by the right hand of God, in which man should walk with dignity.

Petition for Woman's Suffrage from the New York Constitutional Convention (1846)[6]

Mr. Greene presented the memorial of six ladies of Jefferson county, asking for the extension of the elective franchise to women. It was read and referred to standing committee No. 4.

The following is the petition:

To the Constitutional Convention of the State of New York:

Your Memorialist inhabitants of Jefferson county, believing that civil government has its foundation in the laws of our existence, as moral and social beings, that the specific object and end of civil government is to protect all in the exercise of all their natural rights, by combining the strength of society for the defence of the individual—believing that the province of civil government is not to create new rights, but to declare and enforce those which originally existed. Believing likewise that all governments must derive their just powers from the consent of the governed "from the great body of society, and not from a favored class, although that favored class may be even a majority of the inhabitants," therefore respectfully represent: That the present government of this state has widely departed from the true democratic principles upon which all just governments must be based by denying to the female portion of community the right of suffrage and any participation in forming the government and laws under which they live, and to which they are amenable, and by imposing upon them burdens of taxation, both directly and indirectly, without admitting them the right of representation, thereby striking down the only safeguards of their individual and personal liberties. Your Memorialists therefore ask your honorable body, to remove this just cause of complaint, by modifying the present Constitution of this State, so as to extend to women equal, and civil and political rights with men. In proposing this change, your petitioners ask you to confer upon them no new right but only to declare and enforce those which they originally inherited, but which have ungenerously been withheld from them, rights, which they as citizens of the state of New York may reasonable and rightfully claim. We might adduce arguments both numerous and decisive in support of our position, but believing that a self-evident truth is sufficiently plain without argument, and in view of our necessarily limited space, we forbear offering any and respectfully submit it for consideration.

Eleanor Vincent,	Susan Ormsby,
Lydia A. Williams,	Amy Ormsby,
Lydia Osborn,	Anna Bishop.

---

6   S. Croswell and R. Sutton, *Report of the Debates and Proceedings of the Convention for the Revision of the Constitution of the State of New York, 1846* (Albany: Albany Argus, 1846), 646.

CHAPTER 10

The Slave Narrative and Antebellum Slave Society

Consider this chapter alongside *Twelve Years a Slave* (2013), a modern cinematic adaptation of a slave narrative first published in 1853. The narrative detailed the saga of a free black northerner named Solomon Northrup who was kidnapped and sold into slavery in 1841. Northrup ultimately escaped and returned to his family in upstate New York but not before enduring twelve years of grueling captivity, coerced labor, and psychological terror. Director Steve McQueen certainly took artistic liberties to bring Northrup's story to the big screen. Critics nonetheless agree that the film stays generally true to Northrup's original narrative and to modern historians' understanding of American slave society before the Civil War.

Like other slave narratives published before the Civil War, *Twelve Years a Slave* provided radical abolitionists with vivid evidence that exposed the horrors of slavery to the American public and especially to the North's rising white middle class. Northup's narrative offered great insight into the effect of slavery not only on the enslaved but on all Americans living in the South. As the former slave turned radical abolitionist Frederick Douglass opined upon the book's initial release, "It is a strange history, its truth far stranger than fiction."[1]

FUNDAMENTALS

1. How did the narrative portray Northrup's life prior to his abduction?

---

[1] "Literary Notices," *Frederick Douglass' Paper* (Rochester, NY), Aug. 5, 1853.

2. Aside from plantation masters, who else profited from Northrup's enslavement?

3. What forms of labor did Northrup and other enslaved persons perform?

4. How did the white men and women depicted in this story attempt to exercise control over enslaved people?

5. What modes did masters and overseers employ to motivate work and improve productivity on the plantation?

ANALYSIS AND INTERPRETATION

1. How were Northrup and other enslaved people able to survive? Why did it take Northrup twelve years to escape?

2. To what extent did Northrup resist his masters' authority? What were the consequences of his resistance?

3. Why was Patsee such an important character in Northrup's narrative? What did her saga reveal about the particular experiences of enslaved women?

4. What critiques of slavery and slave society are present in Northrup's narrative? In particular, how did it portray the effects of slavery on white men and women?

5. How did *Twelve Years a Slave* portray the economic significance of slavery? To what extent did antebellum slavery mesh well with the ascendant values of market capitalism?

6. To what extent is empire on display in this film? What was the relationship of slavery to the expansion of American empire in the nineteenth century?

CHAPTER 11

Free Society, Slave Society, and the Promise of the West

I n the decade following 1845, the United States embarked on a period of aggressive western expansion, adding its first states and territories on the Pacific coast and organizing the vast interior from Texas to the Canadian border. Imperial conquest coincided with economic growth. Thousands of miles of new railroad track connected the growing cities of the Great Lakes to the Northeast; production boomed in mining and manufacturing; and the value of slave-produced cotton exploded, fueling industrialization in the North and Britain.

This expanding empire was also dividing. Territorial acquisition provoked repeated crises over the future of slavery in the West. At stake was not only the balance of power in Congress between free states and slave states but also whether northern free labor or southern slavery would define the future of the United States.

Congress's attempts to address these crises tended to enflame tensions. The Kansas-Nebraska Act of 1854 may have been the most divisive such attempt. Among other consequences, it convinced northerners, including Abraham Lincoln, that a "slave power" conspiracy was plotting to spread slavery west and even reintroduce it to the North. Lincoln's speech against the Kansas-Nebraska Act in Peoria, Illinois is widely considered a launching point for his career in national politics that would bring him to the presidency in 1861.

In the midst of the sectional crisis, northern and southern intellectuals considered the relative merits of free labor and slave society. Proslavery southern intellectuals such as George Fitzhugh defended what they saw as the benevolent paternalism of slavery while criticizing northern capitalism's coercive destructiveness. Although hostile to slavery, Henry David Thoreau was among the northern intellectuals—known as Transcendentalists—who doubted the freedom offered by market society. From the relative isolation of Walden Pond in Concord, Massachusetts, Thoreau offered a critical assessment of life within the North's so-called free society.

FUNDAMENTALS

1. Why did Lincoln oppose the repeal of the Missouri Compromise? What potential consequences of the Kansas-Nebraska Act did he identify?

2. Lincoln compared the "spirit of '76" with the "spirit of Nebraska." What did he mean by that comparison? Did he believe the two "spirits" were compatible?

3. According to Fitzhugh, what "virtues" defined "free" society?

4. What developments in northern society did Thoreau criticize? What alternatives did he propose?

ANALYSIS AND INTERPRETATION

1. What was Lincoln's vision for the American West? How might slavery's expansion have threatened that vision?

2. To what extent was Lincoln an abolitionist? How would you characterize his views on slavery, African Americans, and the rights of slaveholders?

3. Why did Fitzhugh believe southern slave society was superior to "free society" in the North? Might there have been any truth in his critique of "free society"?

4. According to Fitzhugh, what values shaped the antebellum southern economy? To what extent might we describe these values as "capitalistic"?

5. According to Thoreau, what aspects of northern society led people to "lead lives of quiet desperation"?

6. Would Thoreau have characterized northern society as "free"? Why or why not?

Abraham Lincoln, "Speech in Peoria, Illinois, on the Kansas-Nebraska Act" (1854)[1]

Preceding the Presidential election of 1852, each of the great political parties, Democrats and Whigs, met in convention and adopted resolutions endorsing the compromise of '50; as a "finality," a final settlement, so far as these parties could make it so, of all slavery agitation.

During this long period of time Nebraska had remained, substantially an uninhabited country, but now emigration to, and settlement within it began to take place. It is about one third as large as the present United States, and its importance so long overlooked, begins to come into view. The restriction of slavery by the Missouri Compromise directly applies to it; in fact, was first made, and has since been maintained, expressly for it ... On January 4th, 1854, Judge [Stephen] Douglas introduces a new bill to give Nebraska territorial government. ... Also, about a month after the introduction of the bill, on the judge's own motion, it is so amended as to declare the Missouri Compromise inoperative and void; and, substantially, that the People who go and settle there may establish slavery, or exclude it, as they may see fit. In this shape the bill passed both branches of congress, and became a law.

This is the *repeal* of the Missouri Compromise. I think, and shall try to show, that it is wrong; wrong in its direct effect, letting slavery into Kansas and Nebraska—and wrong in its prospective principle, allowing it to spread to every other part of the wide world, where men can be found inclined to take it.

This *declared* indifference, but as I must think, covert *real* zeal for the spread of slavery, I can not but hate. I hate it because of the monstrous injustice of slavery itself. I hate it because it deprives our republican example of its just influence in the world—enables the enemies of free institutions, with plausibility, to taunt us as hypocrites—causes the real friends of freedom to doubt our sincerity, and especially because it forces so many really good men amongst ourselves into an open war with the very fundamental principles of civil liberty—criticising the Declaration of Independence, and insisting that there is no right principle of action but *self-interest*.

Before proceeding, let me say I think I have no prejudice against the Southern people. They are just what we would be in their situation. If slavery did not now exist amongst them, they would not introduce it. If it did now exist amongst us, we should not instantly give it up. This I believe of the masses north and south. Doubtless there are individuals, on both sides, who would not hold slaves under any circumstances; and others who would gladly introduce slavery anew, if it were out of existence. We know that some southern men do free their slaves, go north, and become tip-top abolitionists; while some northern ones go south, and become most cruel slave-masters.

When southern people tell us they are no more responsible for the origin of slavery, than we; I acknowledge the fact. When it is said that the institution exists; and that it is very difficult to get rid of it, in any satisfactory way, I can understand and appreciate the saying. I surely will not

---

1 From Arthur Brooks Lapsley, ed., *The Writings of Abraham Lincoln* (New York: G. P. Putnam's Sons, 1906), 188–226.

blame them for not doing what I should not know how to do myself. If all earthly power were given me, I should not know what to do, as to the existing institution. My first impulse would be to free all the slaves, and send them to Liberia,—to their own native land. But a moment's reflection would convince me, that whatever of high hope, (as I think there is) there may be in this, in the long run, its sudden execution is impossible. If they were all landed there in a day, they would all perish in the next ten days; and there are not surplus shipping and surplus money enough in the world to carry them there in many times ten days. What then? Free them all, and keep them among us as underlings? Is it quite certain that this betters their condition? I think I would not hold one in slavery, at any rate; yet the point is not clear enough for me to denounce people upon. What next? Free them, and make them politically and socially, our equals? My own feelings will not admit of this; and if mine would, we well know that those of the great mass of white people will not. Whether this feeling accords with justice and sound judgment, is not the sole question, if indeed, it is any part of it. A universal feeling, whether well or ill-founded, can not be safely disregarded. We can not, then, make them equals. It does seem to me that systems of gradual emancipation might be adopted; but for their tardiness in this, I will not undertake to judge our brethren of the south.

When they remind us of their constitutional rights, I acknowledge them, not grudgingly, but fully, and fairly; and I would give them any legislation for the reclaiming of their fugitives, which should not, in its stringency, be more likely to carry a free man into slavery, than our ordinary criminal laws are to hang an innocent one.

But all this; to my judgment, furnishes no more excuse for permitting slavery to go into our own free territory, than it would for reviving the African slave trade by law. The law which forbids the bringing of slaves *from* Africa; and that which has so long forbid the taking them *to* Nebraska, can hardly be distinguished on any moral principle; and the repeal of the former could find quite as plausible excuses as that of the latter.

Some men, mostly Whigs, who condemn the repeal of the Missouri Compromise, nevertheless hesitate to go for its restoration, lest they be thrown in company with the abolitionist. Will they allow me as an old Whig to tell them good humoredly, that I think this is very silly? Stand with anybody that stands RIGHT. Stand with him while he is right and PART with him when he goes wrong. Stand WITH the abolitionist in restoring the Missouri Compromise; and stand AGAINST him when he attempts to repeal the fugitive slave law. In the latter case you stand with the southern disunionist. What of that? you are still right. In both cases you are right. In both cases you oppose the dangerous extremes. In both you stand on middle ground and hold the ship level and steady. In both you are national and nothing less than national. This is good old Whig ground. To desert such ground, because of any company, is to be less than a Whig—less than a man—less than an American.

I particularly object to the NEW position which the avowed principle of this Nebraska law gives to slavery in the body politic. I object to it because it assumes that there CAN be MORAL RIGHT in the enslaving of one man by another. I object to it as a dangerous dalliance for a few free people—a sad evidence that, feeling prosperity we forget right—that liberty, as a principle, we have ceased to revere. I object to it because the fathers of the republic eschewed, and rejected it. The argument of "Necessity" was the only argument they ever admitted in favor of slavery; and so far, and so far only as it carried them, did they ever go. They found the institution existing among us, which they could not help; and they cast blame upon the British King for having permitted its introduction. BEFORE the constitution, they prohibited its introduction into the north-western Territory—the only country we owned, then free from it. AT the framing and adoption of the constitution, they forbore to so much as mention the word "slave" or "slavery" in the whole instrument. In the provision for the recovery of fugitives, the slave is spoken of as a "PERSON HELD TO SERVICE OR LABOR." In that prohibiting the abolition of the African slave trade for twenty years, that trade is spoken of as "The migration or importation of such persons as any of the States NOW EXISTING, shall think proper to admit," &c. These are the only provisions alluding to slavery. Thus, the thing is hid away, in the constitution, just as an afflicted man hides away a wen or a cancer, which he dares not cut out at once, lest he bleed to death; with the promise, nevertheless, that the cutting may begin at the end of a given time. Less than this our fathers COULD not do; and NOW [MORE?] they WOULD not do. Necessity drove them so far, and farther, they would not go. But this is not all. The earliest Congress, under the constitution, took the same view of slavery. They hedged and hemmed it in to the narrowest limits of necessity.

Thus we see, the plain unmistakable spirit of that age, towards slavery, was hostility to the PRINCIPLE, and toleration, ONLY BY NECESSITY.

But NOW it is to be transformed into a "sacred right." Nebraska brings it forth, places it on the high road to extension and perpetuity; and, with a pat on its back, says to it, "Go, and God speed you." Henceforth it is to be the chief jewel of the nation—the very figure-head of the ship of State. Little by little, but steadily as man's march to the grave, we have been giving up the OLD for the NEW faith. Near eighty years ago we began by declaring that all men are created equal; but now from that beginning we have run down to the other declaration, that for SOME men to enslave OTHERS is a "sacred right of self-government." These principles can not stand together. They are as opposite as God and mammon; and whoever holds to the one, must despise the other.

Let no one be deceived. The spirit of seventy-six and the spirit of Nebraska, are utter antagonisms; and the former is being rapidly displaced by the latter.

Fellow countrymen—Americans south, as well as north, shall we make no effort to arrest this? Already the liberal party throughout the world, express the apprehension "that the one retrograde institution in America, is undermining the principles of progress, and fatally violating the noblest political system the world ever saw." This is not the taunt of enemies, but the warning of friends. Is it quite safe to disregard it—to despise it? Is there no danger to liberty itself, in discarding the earliest practice, and first precept of our ancient faith? In our greedy chase to make profit of the negro, let us beware, lest we "cancel and tear to pieces" even the white man's charter of freedom.

Our republican robe is soiled, and trailed in the dust. Let us repurify it. Let us turn and wash it white, in the spirit, if not the blood, of the Revolution. Let us turn slavery from its claims of "moral right," back upon its existing legal rights, and its arguments of "necessity." Let us return it to the position our fathers gave it; and there let it rest in peace. Let us re-adopt the Declaration of Independence, and with it, the practices, and policy, which harmonize with it. Let north and south—let all Americans—let all lovers of liberty everywhere—join in the great and good work. If we do this, we shall not only have saved the Union; but we shall have so saved it, as to make, and to keep it, forever worthy of the saving. We shall have so saved it, that the succeeding millions of free happy people, the world over, shall rise up, and call us blessed, to the latest generations.

George Fitzhugh, *Sociology for the South,*
or the Failure of Free Society (1854)[2]

Liberty and equality are new things under the sun. The free states of antiquity abounded with slaves. The feudal system that supplanted Roman institutions changed the form of slavery, but brought with it neither liberty nor equality. France and the Northern States of our Union have alone fully and fairly tried the experiment of a social organization founded upon universal liberty and equality of rights. In France and in our Northern States the experiment has already failed, if we are to form our opinions from the discontent of the masses, or to believe the evidence of the Socialists, Communists, Anti-Renters, and a thousand other agrarian sects that have arisen in these countries, and threaten to subvert the whole social fabric ... [L]iberty and equality have not conduced to enhance the comfort or the happiness of the people. Crime and pauperism have increased. Riots, trades unions, strikes for higher wages, discontent breaking out into revolution, are things of daily occurrence, and show that the poor see and feel quite as clearly as the philosophers, that their condition is far worse under the new than under the old order of things. ...

The struggle to better one's condition, to pull others down or supplant them, is the great organic law of free society. All men being equal, all aspire to the highest honors and the largest possessions. Good men and bad men teach their children one and the same lesson—"Go ahead, push your way in the world." In such society, virtue, if virtue there be, loses all her loveliness because of her selfish aims. None but the selfish virtues are encouraged, because none other aid a man in the race of free competition. Good men and bad men have the same end in view, are in pursuit of the same object—self-promotion, self-elevation. The good man is prudent, cautious, and cunning of fence; he knows well the arts (the virtues, if you please,) which will advance his fortunes and enable him to press and supplant others; he bides his time, takes advantage of the follies, the improvidence, and vices of others, and makes his fortune out of the misfortunes of his fellow men. The bad man is rash, hasty, and unskillful. He is equally selfish, but not half so cunning. Selfishness is almost the only motive of human conduct with good and bad in free society, where every man is taught that he may change and better his condition. A vulgar adage, "Every man for himself, and devil take the hindmost," is the moral which liberty and free competition inculcate. Now, there are no more honors and wealth in proportion to numbers, in this generation, than in the one which preceded it; population fully keeps pace with the means of subsistence; hence, those who better their condition or rise to higher places in society, do so generally by pulling down others or pushing them from their places. Where men of strong minds, of strong wills, and of great self-control, come into free competition with the weak and improvident, the latter soon become the inmates of jails and penitentiaries. ... The bestowing upon men equality of rights, is but giving license to the strong to oppress the weak. It begets the grossest inequalities of condition.

---

2 From George Fitzhugh, *Sociology for the South: Or the Failure of Free Society* (Richmond: A. Morris, 1854), 226–227; 229–230; 233; 253–255.

There is no rivalry, no competition to get employment among slaves, as among free laborers. Nor is there a war between master and slave. The master's interest prevents his reducing the slaves allowance or wages in infancy or sickness, for he might lose the slave by so doing. His feeling for his slave never permits him to stint him in old age. The slaves are all well fed, well clad, have plenty of fuel, and are happy. They have no dread of the future—no fear of want. A state of dependence is the only condition in which reciprocal affection can exist among human beings— the only situation in which the war of competition ceases, and peace, amity and good will arise. A state of independence always begets more or less of jealous rivalry and hostility. A man loves his children because they are weak, helpless and dependent; he loves his wife for similar reasons. ...

~~~

At the slaveholding South all is peace, quiet, plenty and contentment. We have no mobs, no trades unions, no strikes for higher wages, no armed resistance to the law, but little jealousy of the rich by the poor. We have but few in our jails, and fewer in our poor houses. We produce enough of the comforts and necessaries of life for a population three or four times as numerous as ours. We are wholly exempt from the torrent of pauperism, crime, agrarianism, and infidelity which Europe is pouring from her jails and alms houses on the already crowded North. Population increases slowly, wealth rapidly. In the tide water region of Eastern Virginia, as far as our experience extends, the crops have doubled in fifteen years, whilst the population has been almost stationary. In the same period the lands, owing to improvements of the soil and the many fine houses erected in the country, have nearly doubled in value. This ratio of improvement has been approximated or exceeded wherever in the South slaves are numerous. We have enough for the present, and no Malthusian spectres frightening us for the future. Wealth is more equally distributed than at the North, where a few millionaires own most of the property of the country. (These millionaires are men of cold hearts and weak minds; they know how to make money, but not how to use it, either for the benefit of themselves or of others.) High intellectual and moral attainments, refinement of head and heart, give standing to a man in the South, however poor he may be. Money is, with few exceptions, the only thing that ennobles at the North. We have poor among us, but none who are over-worked and under-fed. We do not crowd cities because lands are abundant and their owners kind, merciful and hospitable. The poor are as hospitable as the rich, the negro as the white man. Nobody dreams of turning a friend, a relative, or a stranger from his door. The very negro who deems it no crime to steal, would scorn to sell his hospitality. We have no loafers, because the poor relative or friend who borrows our horse, or spends a week under our roof, is a welcome guest. The loose economy, the wasteful mode of living at the South, is a blessing when rightly considered; it keeps want, scarcity and famine at a distance, because it leaves room for retrenchment. The nice, accurate economy of France, England and New England, keeps society always on the verge of famine, because it leaves no room to retrench, that is to live on a part only of what they now consume. Our society exhibits no appearance of precocity, no symptoms of decay. A long course of continuing improvement is in prospect before us, with no limits which human foresight can descry. Actual liberty and equality with our white population has been approached much nearer than in the free States. Few of our whites ever work as day laborers, none as cooks, scullions, ostlers, body servants, or in other menial capacities. One free citizen does not lord it over another; hence that feeling of independence and equality that distinguishes us; hence that pride of character, that self-respect, that gives us ascendancy when we come in contact with Northerners. It is a distinction to be a Southerner, as it was once to be a Roman citizen.

Henry David Thoreau, *Walden* (1854)[3]

The mass of men lead lives of quiet desperation. What is called resignation is confirmed desperation. From the desperate city you go into the desperate country, and have to console yourself with the bravery of minks and muskrats. A stereotyped but unconscious despair is concealed even under what are called the games and amusements of mankind. There is no play in them, for this comes after work. But it is a characteristic of wisdom not to do desperate things. ...

The greater part of what my neighbors call good I believe in my soul to be bad, and if I repent of anything, it is very likely to be my good behavior. What demon possessed me that I behaved so well? You may say the wisest thing you can, old man—you who have lived seventy years, not without honor of a kind—I hear an irresistible voice which invites me away from all that. One generation abandons the enterprises of another like stranded vessels.

I think that we may safely trust a good deal more than we do. We may waive just so much care of ourselves as we honestly bestow elsewhere. Nature is as well adapted to our weakness as to our strength. ...

Let us consider for a moment what most of the trouble and anxiety which I have referred to is about, and how much it is necessary that we be troubled, or at least careful. It would be some advantage to live a primitive and frontier life, though in the midst of an outward civilization, if only to learn what are the gross necessaries of life and what methods have been taken to obtain them; or even to look over the old day-books of the merchants, to see what it was that men most commonly bought at the stores, what they stored, that is, what are the grossest groceries. For the improvements of ages have had but little influence on the essential laws of man's existence; as our skeletons, probably, are not to be distinguished from those of our ancestors.

By the words, *necessary of life*, I mean whatever, of all that man obtains by his own exertions, has been from the first, or from long use has become, so important to human life that few, if any, whether from savageness, or poverty, or philosophy, ever attempt to do without it. ...

Most of the luxuries, and many of the so-called comforts of life, are not only not indispensable, but positive hindrances to the elevation of mankind. With respect to luxuries and comforts, the wisest have ever lived a more simple and meagre life than the poor. The ancient philosophers, Chinese, Hindoo, Persian, and Greek, were a class than which none has been poorer in outward riches, none so rich in inward. ...

~~~

I went to the woods because I wished to live deliberately, to front only the essential facts of life, and see if I could not learn what it had to teach, and not, when I came to die, discover that I had not lived. I did not wish to live what was not life, living is so dear; nor did I wish to practise resignation, unless it was quite necessary. I wanted to live deep and suck out all the marrow of life, to cut a broad swath and shave close, to drive life into a corner, and reduce it to its lowest terms, and, if it proved to be mean, why then to get the whole and genuine meanness of it, and publish its

---

3   From Henry David Thoreau, *Walden*, ed. J. Milnor Dorey (New York: C. E. Merrill Co., 1910), 37; 40; 41–42; 44–45; 134–137.

meanness to the world; or if it were sublime, to know it by experience, and be able to give a true account of it in my next excursion. For most men, it appears to me, are in a strange uncertainty about it, whether it is of the devil or of God, and have somewhat hastily concluded that it is the chief end of man here to "glorify God and enjoy him forever."

Still we live meanly, like ants; though the fable tells us that we were long ago changed into men; like pygmies we fight with cranes; it is error upon error, and clout upon clout, and our best virtue has for its occasion a superfluous and inevitable wretchedness. Our life is frittered away by detail. An honest man has hardly need to count more than his ten fingers, or in extreme cases he may add his ten toes, and lump the rest. Simplicity, simplicity, simplicity! I say, let your affairs be as two or three, and not a hundred or a thousand; instead of a million, count half a dozen, and keep your accounts on your thumb nail. ... Simplify, simplify. Instead of three meals a day, if it be necessary eat but one; instead of a hundred dishes, five; and reduce other things in proportion. ...

... The nation itself, with all its so-called internal improvements, which, by the way, are all external and superficial, is just such an unwieldy and overgrown establishment, cluttered with furniture and tripped up by its own traps, ruined by luxury and heedless expense, by want of calculation and a worthy aim, as the million households in the land; and the only cure for them is in a rigid economy, a stern and more than Spartan simplicity of life and elevation of purpose. It lives too fast. Men think that it is essential that the Nation have commerce, and export ice, and talk through a telegraph, and ride thirty miles an hour, without a doubt, whether they do or not; but whether we should live like baboons or like men, is a little uncertain.

If we do not get out sleepers, and forge rails, and devote days and nights to the work, but go tinkering upon our lives to improve them, who will build railroads? And if railroads are not built, how shall we get to heaven in season? But if we stay at home and mind our business, who will want railroads? We do not ride on the railroad; it rides upon us. Did you ever think what those sleepers are that underlie the railroad? Each one is a man, an Irishman, or a Yankee man. The rails are laid on them, and they are covered with sand, and the cars run smoothly over them. They are sound sleepers, I assure you. And every few years a new lot is laid down and run over; so that if some have the pleasure of riding on a rail, others have the misfortune to be ridden upon.

Why should we live with such a hurry and waste of life? We are determined to be starved before we are hungry. Men say that a stitch in time saves nine, and so they take a thousand stitches today to save nine tomorrow.

CHAPTER 12

Reconstructing Democracy, Consolidating Empire

I n the Gettysburg Address, Abraham Lincoln called upon Americans to complete the "unfinished work" of the Civil War. Only by ensuring that the nation experienced "a new birth of freedom," he announced, would American democracy survive. But what did freedom mean? Who would enjoy its fruits? Who would be part of the American nation, and on what terms? In the years following the Civil War, policymakers, freedpeople, immigrants, Native Americans, and myriad others struggled with these questions, offering distinct visions of American democracy in the process.

The abolition of slavery and the reconstruction of the South posed formidable challenges. As over four million freedpeople sought to realize their own visions of freedom, defiant southern whites fought to preserve white supremacy and limit the significance of emancipation. The South's transition to free labor and interracial democracy would proceed with rancor, violence, and, for most freedpeople, catastrophic disappointment.

Union victory also ended the antebellum debate over whether the future of the American West would be slave or free. As they oversaw the Union's reconstruction, Republican leaders consolidated America's continental empire and secured the West for white settlement and capitalist enterprise. Native American nations, such as the Apaches, Nez Perce, and Sioux, responded by defending their traditional ways and by impeding easy conquest.

By the end of the 1870s, Lincoln's "new birth of freedom" seemed chimerical for most African Americans, Native Americans, and, increasingly, Chinese immigrants who had fueled economic development in the Pacific West. The consolidated empire and the concomitant rise of industrial capitalism propelled the United States toward the pinnacle of global economic power. Yet the freedom and equality that many saw as the promise of American democracy remained tragically unfulfilled.

FUNDAMENTALS

1. Based on these readings, what political and economic problems did the United States face after the Civil War?

2. What did the freedpeople of Edisto Island seek to achieve with their petition?

3. According to Schurz, how had emancipation transformed race relations in the South?

4. What future did Walker envision for Native Americans in the West? What evidence did he use to support his conclusions?

5. What groups of Americans were represented in Thomas Nast's cartoon?

ANALYSIS AND INTERPRETATION

1. What did Lincoln mean by a "new birth of freedom"? How did others understand the meaning of freedom in the late nineteenth century?

2. Why might land ownership have figured so prominently in the vision of freedom held by the freedpeople of Edisto Island?

3. Did Schurz believe that egalitarian race relations would take hold in the post-emancipation South? Why or why not?

4. How did Francis Amasa Walker's hopes for the Native Americans in the West compare to the southern freedpeople's vision of the future?

5. To what extent was the Civil War a war for empire? How would you characterize the political, social, and economic goals that drove American empire after the Civil War?

6. How did Thomas Nast view immigration restriction? How did he link restriction of the Chinese with experiences of other groups?

Abraham Lincoln, *Gettysburg Address* (1863)[1]

Four score and seven years ago our fathers brought forth on this continent, a new nation, conceived in Liberty, and dedicated to the proposition that all men are created equal.

Now we are engaged in a great civil war, testing whether that nation, or any nation so conceived and so dedicated, can long endure. We are met on a great battle-field of that war. We have come to dedicate a portion of that field, as a final resting place for those who here gave their lives that that nation might live. It is altogether fitting and proper that we should do this.

But, in a larger sense, we can not dedicate—we can not consecrate—we can not hallow—this ground. The brave men, living and dead, who struggled here, have consecrated it, far above our poor power to add or detract. The world will little note, nor long remember what we say here, but it can never forget what they did here. It is for us the living, rather, to be dedicated here to the unfinished work which they who fought here have thus far so nobly advanced. It is rather for us to be here dedicated to the great task remaining before us—that from these honored dead we take increased devotion to that cause for which they gave the last full measure of devotion—that we here highly resolve that these dead shall not have died in vain—that this nation, under God, shall have a new birth of freedom—and that government of the people, by the people, for the people, shall not perish from the earth.

---

1 From John George Nicolay and John Hay, *Abraham Lincoln: A History, vol. 8* (New York: Century Company, 1890), 200–201.

Committee of Freedmen on Edisto Island, South Carolina to President Andrew Johnson (1865)[2]

To the President of the United States. We the freedmen of Edisto Island South Carolina have learned From you through Major General OO Howard Commissioner of the Freedman's Bureau. With deep sorrow and Painful hearts of the possibility of government restoring These lands to the former owners. We are well aware Of the many perplexing and trying questions that burden Your mind. And do therefore pray to god (the preserver of all, and who has through our Late and beloved President (Lincoln) proclamation and the war made Us A free people) that he may guide you in making Your decisions, and give you that wisdom that Cometh from above to settle these great and Important Questions for the best interests of the country and the Colored race: Here is where succession was born and Nurtured. Here is where we have toiled nearly all Our lives as slaves and were treated like dumb Driven cattle. This is our home, we have made These lands what they are, we were the only true and loyal people that were found in possession of these Lands, we have been always ready to strike for Liberty and humanity yea to fight if needs be To preserve this glorious union. Shall not we who Are freedman and have been always true to this Union have the same rights as are enjoyed by Others? Have we broken any Law of these United States? Have we forfeited our rights of our property In Land?—If not then are not our rights as A free people and good citizens of these United States To be considered before the rights of those who were Found in rebellion against this good and just Government (and now being conquered) come (as they Seem) with penitent hearts and beg forgiveness For past offences and also ask if their lands Cannot be restored to them are these rebellious Spirits to be reinstate in their possessions And we who have been abused and oppressed For many long years not to be allowed the Privilege of purchasing land But be subject To the will of these large Land owners? God forbid. Land monopoly is injurious to the advancement of the course of freedom, and if Government Does not make some provision by which we as Freedmen can obtain A Homestead, we have Not bettered our condition.

We have been encouraged by Government to take Up these lands in small tracts, receiving Certificates of the same—we have thus far Taken sixteen thousand (16000) acres of Land here on This Island. We are ready to pay for this land When Government calls for it, and now after What has been done will the good and just Government take from us all this right and make us subject to the will of those who have cheated and Oppressed us for many years God forbid!

---

2   Henry Bram et al., "Committee of Freedmen on Edisto Island, South Carolina to President Andrew Johnson," *Letters Received*, series 15, Washington Headquarters, Bureau of Refugees, Freedmen, & Abandoned Lands, Record Group 105, National Archives. 1865.

Guided by General William T. Sherman's order of January 1865, the freedpeople of Edisto Island, South Carolina settled upon abandoned plantations and expected to gain ownership of forty-acre plots. In October 1865, however, President Andrew Johnson ordered General Oliver Otis Howard, head of the Freedmen's Bureau, to inform the Edisto Islanders that the former white owners would have their property restored. The freedpeople would lose their land and be forced to work for wages. In response, the Edisto Islanders crafted this protest addressed to President Johnson.

We the freedmen of this Island and of the State of South Carolina—Do therefore petition to you as the President of these United States, that some provisions be made by which Every colored man can purchase land and Hold it as his own. We wish to have A home if It be but a few acres, without some provision is Made our future is sad to look upon, yes our Situation is dangerous. We therefore look to you In this trying hour as A true friend of the poor and Neglected race. For protection and Equal rights, with the privilege of purchasing A Homestead—A Homestead right here in the Heart of South Carolina.

We pray that God will direct your heart in Making such provision for us as freedmen which Will tend to unite these states together stronger Than ever before—May God bless you in the Administration of your duties as the President Of these United States in the humble prayer Of us all.—

In behalf of the Freedmen
Henry Bram
Ishmael Moultrie
Yates Sampson

Carl Schurz, *Report on the Condition of the South* (1865)[3]

... I mentioned above that all organized attacks upon our military forces stationed in the south have ceased; but there are still localities where it is unsafe for a man wearing the federal uniform or known as an officer of the government to be abroad outside of the immediate reach of our garrisons. ... [N]o instance has come to my notice in which the people of a city or a rural distinct cordially fraternized with the army. Here and there the soldiers were welcomed as protectors against apprehended dangers; but general exhibitions of cordiality on the part of the population I have not heard of. ... upon the whole, the soldier of the Union is still looked upon as a stranger, an intruder—as the "Yankee," "the enemy." ...

While the generosity and toleration shown by the [United States] government to the people lately in rebellion has not met with a corresponding generosity shown by those people to the government's friends, it has brought forth some results which, if properly developed, will become of value. It has facilitated the re-establishment of the forms of civil government, and led many of those who had been active in the rebellion to take part in the act of bringing back the States to their constitutional relations ... There is, at present, no danger of another insurrection ... and the people are willing to reconstruct their State governments, and to send their senators and representatives to Congress.

But as to the moral value of these results, we must not indulge in any delusions. There are two principal points to which I beg to call your attention. In the first place, the rapid return to power and influence of so many of those who but recently were engaged in a bitter war against the Union, has had an effect which was certainly not originally contemplated by the government. Treason does, under existing circumstances, not appear odious in the south. The people are not impressed with any sense of its criminality. And, secondly, there is, as yet, among the southern people an utter absence of national feeling. I made it a business, while in the south, to watch the symptoms of "returning loyalty" as they appeared not only in private conversation, but in the public press and in the speeches delivered and the resolutions passed at Union meetings. Hardly ever was there an expression of hearty attachment to this great republic, or an appeal to the impulses of patriotism; but whenever submission to the national authority was declared and advocated, it was almost uniformly placed upon two principal grounds: That, under present circumstances, the southern people could "do no better;" and then that submission was the only means by which they could rid themselves of the federal soldiers and obtain once more control of their own affairs. ...

---

3   From Carl Schurz, "Report of Carl Schurz on the States of South Carolina, Georgia, Alabama, Mississippi, and Louisiana," in Carl Schurz and U.S. Grant, *Message of the President of the United States: Communicating, in Compliance with a Resolution of the Senate of the 12th Instant, Information in Relation to the States of the Union Lately in Rebellion, Accompanied by a Report of Carl Schurz on the States of South Carolina, Georgia, Alabama, Mississippi, and Louisiana; Also a Report of Lieutenant General Grant, on the Same Subject* (Washington, DC: U.S. Government Printing Office, 1865), 7–21.

Born in the German Rhineland, Carl Schurz came to the U.S. in 1852 and became a prominent member of the Republican Party in Wisconsin. Schurz fought for the North, serving as a general in the Union army. Andrew Johnson, who became president after Lincoln's assassination, sent Schurz to assess conditions in the South in the summer of 1865. This report, presented to Congress in December 1865, was the product of Schurz's extensive observations.

In speaking above of the improbability of an insurrectionary movement on a large scale, I did not mean to say that I considered resistance in detail to the execution of the laws of Congress and the measures of the government impossible. ... [M]ost of the conversations I had with southerners upon this subject led me to apprehend that they ... are rather inclined to ask money of the government as compensation for their emancipated slaves, for the rebuilding of the levees on the Mississippi, and various kinds of damage done by our armies for military purposes, than, as the current expression is, to "help paying the expenses of the whipping they have received." In fact, there are abundant indications in newspaper articles, public speeches, and electioneering documents of candidates which render it eminently probable that on the claim of compensation for their emancipated slaves the southern States, as soon as readmitted to representation in Congress, will be almost a unit. In the Mississippi convention the idea was broached by Mr. Potter, in an elaborate speech, to have the late slave States relieved from taxation "for years to come," in consideration of "debt due them" for the emancipated slaves; and this plea I have frequently heard advocated in private conversations. ...

... In at least nineteen cases of twenty the reply I received to my inquiry about their views on the new system was uniformly this: "You cannot make the negro work, without physical compulsion." I heard this hundreds of times, heard it wherever I went, heard it in nearly the same words from so many different persons, that at last I came to the conclusion that this is the prevailing sentiment among the southern people. ...

... I found but few people who were willing to make due allowance for the adverse influence of exceptional circumstances. By a large majority of those I came in contact with, and they mostly belonged to the more intelligent class, every irregularity that occurred was directly charged against the system of free labor. If negroes walked away from the plantations, it was conclusive proof of the incorrigible instability of the negro, and the impracticability of free negro labor. If some individual negroes violated the terms of their contract, it proved unanswerably that no negro had, or ever would have, a just conception of the binding force of a contract, and that this system of free negro labor was bound to be a failure. If some negroes shirked, or did not perform their task with sufficient alacrity, it was produced as irrefutable evidence to show that physical compulsion was actually indispensable to make the negro work. If negroes, idlers or refugees crawling about the towns, applied to the authorities for subsistence, it was quoted as incontestably establishing the point that the negro was too improvident to take care of himself, and must necessarily be consigned to the care of a master. I heard a Georgia planter argue most seriously that one of his negroes had shown himself certainly unfit for freedom because he impudently refused to submit to a whipping. ... It frequently struck me that persons who conversed about every other subject calmly and sensibly would lose their temper as soon as the negro question was touched.

A belief, conviction, or prejudice, or whatever you may call it, so widely spread and apparently so deeply rooted as this, that the negro will not work without physical compulsion, is certainly calculated to have a very serious influence upon the conduct of the people entertaining it. It naturally produced a desire to preserve slavery in its original form as much and as long as possible ... remember the admission made by one of the provisional governors, over two months after the close of the war, that the people of his State still indulged in a lingering hope slavery might yet be preserved—or to introduce into the new system that element of physical compulsion which would make the negro work. Efforts were, indeed, made to hold the negro in his old state of subjection, especially in such localities where our military forces had not yet penetrated, or where the country was not garrisoned in detail. Here and there planters succeeded for a limited period to keep their former slaves in ignorance, or at least doubt, about their new rights; but the main agency employed for that purpose was force and intimidation. In many instances negroes who walked away from the plantations, or were found upon the roads, were shot or otherwise severely punished, which was calculated to produce the impression among those remaining with their masters that an attempt to escape from slavery would result in certain destruction. A large proportion of the many acts of violence committed is undoubtedly attributable to this motive. ...

The conviction, however, that slavery in the old form cannot be maintained has forced itself upon the minds of many of those who ardently desired its preservation. But while the necessity of a new system was recognized as far as the right of property in the individual negro is concerned, many attempts were made to introduce into that new system the element of physical compulsion, which ... is so generally considered indispensable. This was done by simply adhering ... as much as possible to the traditions of the old system, even where the relations between employers and laborers had been fixed by contract. The practice of corporal punishment was still continued to a great extent ... The habit is so inveterate with a great many persons as to render, on the least provocation, the impulse to whip a negro almost irresistible. It will continue to be so until the southern people will have learned, so as never to forget it, that a black man has rights which a white man is bound to respect.

Here I will insert some remarks on the general treatment of the blacks as a class, from the whites as a class. It is not on the plantations and at the hands of the planters themselves that the negroes have to suffer the greatest hardships. Not only the former slaveholders, but the non-slaveholding whites, who, even previous to the war, seemed to be more ardent in their pro-slavery feelings than the planters themselves, are possessed by a singularly bitter and vindictive feeling against the colored race since the negro ceased to be property. The pecuniary value which the individual negro formerly represented having disappeared, the maiming and killing of colored men seems to be looked upon by many as one of those venial offences which must be forgiven to the outraged feelings of a wronged and robbed people. Besides, the services rendered by the negro to the national cause during the war, which make him an object of special interest to the loyal people, make him an object of particular vindictiveness to those whose hearts were set upon the success of the rebellion. The number of murders and assaults perpetrated upon the negroes is very great; we can form only an approximate estimate of what is going on in those parts of the south which are not closely garrisoned, and from which no regular reports are received, by what occurs under the very eyes of our military authorities. ...

... So far, the spirit of persecution has shown itself so strong as to make the protection of the freedman by the military arm of the government in many localities necessary—in almost all, desirable. It must not be forgotten that in a community a majority of whose members is peaceably disposed, but not willing or not able to enforce peace and order, a comparatively small number of bold lawless men can determine the character of the whole. ...

... Aside from the assumption that the negro will not work without physical compulsion, there appears to be another popular notion prevalent in the south, which stands as no less serious an obstacle in the way of a successful solution of the problem. It is that the negro exists for the special object of raising cotton, rice, and sugar for the whites, and that it is illegitimate for him to indulge, like other people, in the pursuit of his own happiness in his own way. Although it is admitted that he has ceased to be the property of a master, it is not admitted that he has a right to become his own master. As Colonel Thomas, assistant commissioner of the Freedmen's Bureau in Mississippi ... very pungently expresses it: "The whites esteem the blacks their property by natural right, and, however much they may admit that the relations of masters and slaves have been destroyed by the war and by the President's emancipation proclamation, they still have an ingrained feeling that the blacks at large belong to the whites at large, and whenever opportunity serves, they treat the colored people just as their profit, caprice or passion may dictate."

Francis Amasa Walker, *Report of the Commissioner of Indian Affairs* (1872)[4]

I have the honor, in conformity with law, to render the annual report on the Indian affairs of the country ... It has seemed desirable, in recognition of the wide popular interest taken in the dealings of the Government with the Indians ... to present at this time a pretty full statement of the situation of Indian affairs, and of the policy of the Government in view of that situation. I have, therefore, ... thrown together as much information as possible ... giving especial prominence to those facts of the situation which may properly go to determine the judgment of the legislator and the private citizen upon the practical questions: What shall be done with the Indian as an obstacle to the progress of settlement and industry? What shall be done with him as a dependent and pensioner on our civilization, when, and so far as, he ceases to oppose or obstruct the extension of railways and of settlement?

THE BEGINNING OF THE END

It belongs ... to a sober view of the situation that three years will see the alternative of war eliminated from the Indian question, and the most powerful and hostile bands of to-day thrown in entire helplessness on the mercy of the Government. Indeed, the progress of two years more, if not of another summer, on the Northern Pacific Railroad will of itself completely solve the great Sioux problem, and leave the ninety thousand Indians ranging between the two transcontinental lines as incapable of resisting the Government as are the Indians of New York or Massachusetts.

SUBMISSION THE ONLY HOPE OF THE INDIANS

No one certainly will rejoice more heartily than the present Commissioner when the Indians of this country cease to be in a position to dictate, in any form or degree, to the Government; when, in fact, the last hostile tribe becomes reduced to the condition of suppliants for charity. This is, indeed, the only hope of salvation for the aborigines of the continent. If they stand up against the progress of civilization and industry, they must be relentlessly crushed. The westward course of population is neither to be denied nor delayed for the sake of all the Indians that ever called this country their home. They must yield or perish; and there is something that savors of providential mercy in the rapidity with which their fate advances upon them, leaving them scarcely the chance to resist before they shall be surrounded and disarmed ... And it is because the present system allows the freest extension of settlement and industry possible under the circumstances, while affording space and time for humane endeavors to rescue the Indian tribes from a position

---

4 From *Annual Report of the Commissioner of Indian Affairs, for the Year 1872* (Washington: U.S. Government Printing Office, 1872), 3–12.

altogether barbarous and incompatible with civilization and social progress, that this system must be approved by all enlightened citizens.

THE CLAIMS OF THE INDIAN

Were the westward course of population to be stayed at the barriers of to-day, ... the Indians would still have hope of life. But another such five years will see the Indians of Dakota and Montana ... reduced to an habitual condition of suffering from want of food.

The freedom of expansion which is working these results is to us of incalculable value. To the Indian it is of incalculable cost. Every year's advance of our frontier takes in a territory as large as some of the kingdoms of Europe. We are richer by hundreds of millions; the Indian is poorer by a large part of the little that he has. This growth is bringing imperial greatness to the nation; to the Indian it brings wretchedness, destitution, beggary. Surely there is obligation found in considerations like these, requiring us in some way, and in the best way, to make good to these original owners of the soil the loss by which we so greatly gain.

Can any principle of national morality be clearer than that, when the expansion and development of a civilized race involve the rapid destruction of the only means of subsistence possessed by the members of a less fortunate race, the higher is bound as of simple right to provide for the lower some substitute for the means of subsistence which it has destroyed? That substitute is, of course, best realized, not by systematic gratuities of food and clothing continued beyond a present emergency, but by directing these people to new pursuits which shall be consistent with the progress of civilization upon the continent; helping them over the first rough places on "the white man's road," and, meanwhile, supplying such subsistence as is absolutely necessary during the period of initiation and experiment.

A LEGALIZED REFORMATORY CONTROL NECESSARY

The assistance due to the Indians from the Government ... should not much longer be irrespective of their own efforts. Just so soon as these tribes cease to be formidable, they should be brought distinctly to the realization of the law that if they would eat they must also work. Nor should it be left to their own choices how miserably they will live, in order that they may escape work as much as possible. The Government should extend over them a rigid reformatory discipline, to save them from falling hopelessly into the condition of pauperism and petty crime. Merely to disarm the savages, and to surround them by forces which it is hopeless in them to resist, without exercising over them for a series of years a system of paternal control, requiring them to learn and practice the arts of industry at least until one generation has been fairly started on a course of self-improvement, is to make it pretty much a matter of certainty that by far the larger part of the now roving Indians will become simply vagabonds in the midst of civilization, forming little camps here and there over the face of the Western States, which will be festering sores on the communities near which they are located; the men resorting for a living to basket-making and hog-stealing; the women to fortune-telling and harlotry. No one who looks about him and observes the numbers of our own race who, despite our strong constitutional disposition to labor, the general example of industry, the possession of all the arts and applicances which diminish effort while they multiply results, and the large rewards offered in the constitution of modern society for success in industrial effort, yet sink to the most abject condition from indolence or from vice, can greatly doubt that, unless prompt and vigorous measures are taken by the Government, something like what has been described is to be the fate of the now roving Indians, when they shall be surrounded and disarmed by the extension of our settlements, and deprived of their traditional means of subsistence through the extinction of game. Unused to manual labor, and physically disqualified for it by the habits of the chase, unprovided with tools and implements, without forethought and without self-control, singularly susceptible to evil influences, with strong animal appetites and no intellectual tastes or aspirations to hold those appetites in check, it would be to assume more than would be taken for granted of any white race under the same conditions, to expect that the wild Indians will become industrious and frugal except through a severe course of industrial instruction and exercise, under restraint. The reservation system affords the place for thus dealing with tribes and bands ... It is only necessary that Federal laws ... shall place all the members of this race under a strict reformatory control by the agents of the Government. Especially is it essential that the right of the Government to keep Indians upon the reservations assigned to them, and to arrest and return them whenever they wander away, should be placed beyond dispute. Without this, whenever these people become restive under compulsion to labor, they will break away in their old roving spirit, and stray off in small bands to neighboring communities, upon which they will prey in a petty fashion, by begging and stealing, until they have made themselves so much of a nuisance that the law is invoked against them, or their apprehensions of violence become excited, when they will pass on, to become the pests of other and more distant communities. In a word, in the two hundred and seventy-five thousand Indians west of the Mississippi, the United States have all the elements of a large gypsy population, which will inevitably become a sore, a well-nigh intolerable, affliction to all that region, unless the Government shall provide for their instruction in the arts of life, which can only be done effectually under a pressure not to be resisted or evaded. The right of the Government to do this cannot be seriously questioned. Expressly excluded by the Constitution from citizenship, the Government is only bound in its treatment of them by considerations of present policy and justice. ...

Thomas Nast, "Every Dog (No Distinction of Color) Has Its Day" (1879)[5]

FIGURE 12.1 Every Dog (No Distinction of Color) Has Its Day

Credit

- Fig. 12.1: Thomas Nast, "Every Dog... Has His Day," *Harper's Weekly*, vol. 23, no. 1154. 1879.

5   Thomas Nast, "Every Dog (No Distinction of Color) Has Its Day," *Harper's Weekly*, Feb. 8, 1879.

CPSIA information can be obtained
at www.ICGtesting.com
Printed in the USA
FSHW021710080520
70029FS